Higher Education, Employment and Earnings in Britain

Richard Blundell
Lorraine Dearden
Alissa Goodman
Howard Reed

The Institute for Fiscal Studies
7 Ridgmont Street
London WC1E 7AE

Published by
The Institute for Fiscal Studies
7 Ridgmount Street
London WC1E 7AE
tel. (44) 171 636 3784
fax (44) 171 323 4780
email: mailbox@ifs.org.uk
internet: http//www.ifs.org.uk

Printed by
KKS Printing
The Printworks
12–20 Rosina Street
London E9 6JE

Preface

This report has been financed by the Department for Education and Employment. The views expressed in it are those of the authors alone and not necessarily those of the Department nor of the Institute for Fiscal Studies which has no corporate views. The authors would like to thank James Steel from the Department for his guidance in all stages of the research. They would also like to thank seminar participants at the Institute for Fiscal Studies, and in particular Andrew Dilnot, for constructive comments and criticisms on earlier versions of this report. The ESRC Data Archive and Peter Shephard at City University kindly provided the NCDS data used in this report. The authors would finally like to thank Judith Payne for preparing this report for publication.

Richard Blundell is Research Director of the Institute for Fiscal Studies and a Professor of Economics at University College London.

Lorraine Dearden is a Programme Co-ordinator at the Institute for Fiscal Studies.

Alissa Goodman is a Senior Research Economist at the Institute for Fiscal Studies.

Howard Reed is a Research Economist at the Institute for Fiscal Studies.

Contents

Summary

Introduction

- This study examines the impact of higher education on individuals' employment prospects and wages in the medium to longer term.
- The analysis compares the labour market outcomes of a sample of graduates at age 33 with a sample of similarly-aged non-graduates who had the prospect of continuing on to higher education but did not do so.

The Data

- The data used come from the National Child Development Survey (NCDS), which is a continuing survey of all individuals born in Britain between 3 and 9 March 1958. Since birth, individuals in the NCDS have been surveyed at five different points, the most recent being in 1991 when they were 33 years old. The dataset provides a rich set of information about individuals' backgrounds and abilities. This makes it a very good source of information for measuring the impact of higher education.
- The advantage of using this cohort of individuals, born in 1958, as the basis of study is that they have potentially been in the labour market long enough after graduation for the full returns to their qualifications to be measured.
- The study focuses on a subsample of the NCDS, containing those with at least one A level — those who could have gone on to higher education.

Methodology

- There are a number of potential biases that can arise when measuring the impact of higher education. We have sought to deal with these carefully during the course of this study. In particular, it is important to control for other characteristics of individuals besides their educational attainment that may affect their labour market outcomes.
- The various techniques used in order to measure the returns to higher education correctly are outlined in the main body of the text.

Who Goes on to Higher Education?

- Amongst those with A levels, three-quarters of the men in our sample obtained some kind of higher education qualification by the age of 33. A slightly smaller proportion of our sample of women — about 70 per cent — obtained higher education qualifications.
- Pupils who showed high ability at a young age at school were more likely to become graduates than others.
- Those from more educated or more affluent family backgrounds were also more likely to go on to obtain higher education qualifications from amongst those with A levels. Family background played an even more important role in determining who made it into A levels at all.

Higher Education and Employment Prospects at 33

- Employment rates amongst the men in our sample at age 33 were very high. There was no discernible additional impact of higher education on the probability of employment at 33 for men.

- Women who were graduates were significantly more likely to be in employment at 33 than their non-graduate counterparts. This difference remains after controlling for other differences between women graduates and non-graduates.

Higher Education and Men's Wages at 33

- The wages of men with higher education qualifications were significantly higher at age 33 than those with just A levels.
- Before taking into account any of the other factors that determine wages, men with non-degree higher education qualifications had hourly wages on average 15 per cent higher than those with just A levels; men with first degrees had hourly wages on average 21 per cent higher; and men with higher degrees had, on average, 16 per cent higher wages than those who could have gone on to higher education but did not.
- Taking into account a wide range of other differences between graduates and non-graduates that affect their wages (for example, differing ability), the 'pure' effect of higher education on men's wages is reduced. Depending on the exact model used, the average mark-up from a first degree ranges between 12 and 18 per cent for men.

Higher Education and Women's Wages at 33

- The impact of higher education on women's wages was found to be considerably larger than its impact on men's wages. Women with non-degree higher education qualifications had hourly wages on average 26 per cent higher than those with just A levels; women with first degrees had hourly wages on average 39 per cent higher; and women with higher degrees had, on average, 43 per cent higher wages than this base group.

- Controlling for other factors determining women's wages, the return to a first degree for women was found to be in the range 34 to 38 per cent.
- The key results on the returns to higher education for men and women are summarised in the Summary Table opposite.

Other Issues

- There are few important wage differences between those taking different *subjects* at higher education level.
- Those who entered higher education as *mature students* did less well in terms of wages at 33 than those who went straight on to higher education after school, but still considerably better than those with no higher education qualifications at all.
- Those who *entered higher education but failed* to obtain any qualification had lower wages than those who did not enter higher education at all.
- Those with higher education qualifications typically have spent less time in the labour market than those without, because of the time it takes to complete a course. Taking into account different levels of *experience* between graduates and non-graduates increases the measured wage return to higher education.
- There is a significant additional pay-off for workers who are in professional or managerial occupations (often referred to as *graduate jobs*), both for those who have higher education qualifications and those without.

Higher Education and the Gender Earnings Gap

- The gender wage gap was considerably lower amongst graduates at age 33 than amongst those who were less qualified. Taking into account differences in ability and background, men with just A levels received hourly wages on average 43 per cent higher than similarly-qualified women; men with first degrees had wages on average 23 per cent higher than women with first degrees.

Higher Education and Weekly Earnings

- For men, the estimated return to higher education in terms of *weekly* earnings was slightly higher than the returns in terms of hourly earnings, indicating that, on average, male graduates work longer hours than non-graduates.
- For women, the weekly return to non-degree qualifications is lower than the hourly return, but the weekly return to a first degree is between 2 and 7 percentage points higher than the hourly return.
- The key results are summarised in the table below.

SUMMARY TABLE

Main results

| | Estimated return (%) | | | | | |
| | Men | | | Women | | |
	Non-degree HE	*First degree*	*Higher degree*	*Non-degree HE*	*First degree*	*Higher degree*
Specification 1:						
Hourly wages	15.0	20.8	15.6	26.1	39.1	42.7
Weekly wages	17.2	22.2	17.7	24.0	42.1	53.3
Specification 2:						
Hourly wages	15.5	18.4	14.1	27.2	38.4	40.8
Weekly wages	18.0	19.2	16.0	24.3	41.1	51.8
Specification 3:						
Hourly wages	14.4	17.1	14.4	22.3	36.8	36.8
Weekly wages	16.0	17.1	16.5	16.8	38.8	45.6
Specification 4:						
Hourly wages	13.6	12.2	8.4	21.8	33.7	31.9
Weekly wages	15.0	12.2	10.3	16.9	40.3	46.5

Note: For details of the different specifications, see box overleaf.

Wage equation specifications: controls included in wage equation

1. Higher education dummies only

2. As specification 1
   + Quintiles of maths and reading ability test scores at age seven
   + Region at age 16
   + School type at age 16

3. As specification 2
   + Family background variables (father's and mother's education, father's social class, mother's employment, absence of mother/father, number of siblings, number of older siblings, all in 1974)
   + Demographic variables (proportion of households in local authority with unemployed head of household, head of household in top social class, council tenancy, owner-occupation)
   + Good school attendance in 1974
   + Employer characteristics in 1991 (employer size, union membership dummy, private sector dummy)

4. As specification 3
   + Ability test scores at age 16
   + A level score according to UCCA formula

CHAPTER 1
Introduction

It is widely accepted that understanding the extent of both the private and public benefits of higher education is crucial for future policy development in this important area. This study examines the impact that degree-level qualifications and other higher education qualifications have on the labour market outcomes of individuals in the medium to longer term. In particular, we look at the impact higher education has on the probability of an individual finding employment later in life and also on the wages or private financial returns associated with different types of higher education. The report does not consider the private non-financial returns or the social returns to higher education.

Rather than simply comparing individuals who undertook some form of higher education (HE) with the rest of the population, we instead use as a comparator group those individuals who obtained at least one (and alternatively at least two) A level qualifications but did not proceed into HE. Our aim in doing this is to focus on the subsample of the population who had the prospect of going into HE but (for whatever reason) did not. An important assumption underlying this approach is that, broadly speaking, a person needs at least one A level to be considered for entry into HE. Statistical analysis presented below indicates that this is a reasonable assumption for degree courses, but in the case of non-degree HE qualifications,[1] there is evidence that

---

[1] In this report, non-degree HE qualifications consist of all NVQ Level 4 qualifications except first degrees. See Table A.1 in Appendix A for full details.

many of the entrants do not have A level qualifications. We return to this issue later in the report.

Estimation of the returns to HE (or the impact of HE on employment) is not straightforward, mainly because it is difficult to disentangle the 'pure' effects of time spent in HE and the resulting qualifications obtained on wages (or employment) from the influence of other factors that affect wages (or employment).[2] There are several issues to contend with in this regard. One is the extent to which HE increases wages by increasing human capital (that is, actually enhancing an individual's potential productivity) or the extent to which the HE process merely identifies workers who are more able and/or productive, enables firms to see these workers easily and thus acts as a 'screening' mechanism. We have little to say about the conflict between human capital and screening models of the educational process in this report. The extent to which HE is purely a screening device or productivity-enhancing is crucial in estimating the social returns to education. However, of more concern to us is the danger of arriving at biased estimates of the private returns to HE due to the omission of factors that determine earnings (other than those working directly through HE). Problems that could induce biases include the failure to control for unmeasured individual ability in the regression, measurement error in the HE variable and unmeasured differences in the rate of time preference across the population that affect individual decisions on whether to enter HE. We describe below how the models estimated in this report are designed to correct for these biases as far as is possible. The dataset that we use — the British National Child Development Survey (NCDS) — provides us with a rich

---

[2]In discussing these issues, we focus on the effect of HE on wages, but the same type of issues arise when looking at the impact of HE on employment.

source of information about the backgrounds, educational attainments and labour market outcomes of members of one particular cohort, born in 1958. This dataset has the advantage that it allows us to track individuals' labour market statuses from the time of first leaving school up until the age of 33 and therefore allows us to look directly at the impact of HE on labour market prospects over an extended period of time.

Of course, the context in which school-leavers of today are making decisions about whether to continue beyond the statutory school-leaving age and into HE is rather different from that which participants in the NCDS faced some twenty years ago. Since the mid-1980s, there has been a massive expansion in the numbers of pupils continuing at school beyond 16 and continuing on into HE. More than one-third of young people pass A levels, compared with just over one in six at the time the NCDS cohort was at school. Almost one in three young people now go into full-time HE in Great Britain, compared with one in eight in 1979.[3] This means that there are now many more highly-educated workers entering the labour force every year than when the NCDS cohort went out to work for the first time. The demand conditions for such workers have also altered fundamentally since this cohort entered work. Technological change and increased international trade have meant that the demand for highly-skilled workers has grown alongside the growing participation in HE. The impact of these important labour market changes on the wage outcomes of the NCDS cohort will be reflected in the returns to HE that we measure in this study. However, the extent to which the large influx of new graduates into the job market in the 1990s will affect the returns to the older cohort analysed in this study depends on the relative demand of firms for younger and

---

[3]Source: Department for Education and Employment, 1996.

older graduates and the extent to which young and old graduates are in competition with each other or with their peer groups; these are difficult issues which this report does not address directly. Certainly, ascertaining the potential longer-term returns to HE for younger workers, who will be most affected by the labour market changes that have taken place, is important from a policy perspective. On the other hand, they have not yet been in the work-force long enough for their returns to HE to be assessed fully — it is difficult to believe that the full returns to HE have set in much before an individual's mid-thirties. As such, they will be beyond the scope of this report.[4]

The format of this report is as follows. Chapter 2 describes the main features of the NCDS data along with giving some descriptive analysis of the numbers of men and women entering and completing different types of HE. In Chapter 3, the methodological difficulties of estimating the returns to HE are discussed. Our methodological approach is presented in Chapter 4. Chapter 5 details the results of our study, which broadens out the brief sketch of the issues involved above to consider the following sets of questions:

- What sorts of individuals obtain A level qualifications?
  - What sort of families do they come from?
  - Are their parents more educated, on average, than the parents of children who do not obtain A levels?
- In what ways do individuals who continue on into HE differ from individuals who had the prospect of going on to HE but chose not to?

----

[4]The early returns to HE have been considered by Bryson and Lissenburgh (1996), who use the 1987 Youth Cohort Study to look at the returns to HE in 1994 of a cohort of individuals aged 22–23.

- Do they come from more favourable family backgrounds?
- Are they generally of higher average ability?
- How important is their schooling background?
- Are other factors associated with their earlier childhood experiences important?
- What impact does obtaining different types of HE have on the probability of being employed at the age of 33?
- What impact does obtaining different types of HE have on wages (both hourly and weekly) at the age of 33?
  - Does starting but not finishing a HE course have any benefits?
  - Do people who commence HE courses immediately after completing school have better wage prospects than those individuals who undertake HE courses as mature students?
  - How do the returns to first degrees compare with the returns to other non-degree HE qualifications, on one hand, and higher degrees, on the other?
  - Are the returns to HE homogeneous across different types of people, or are there different returns according to the sex, schooling background, ability or family background of the individual?
  - Does the return to HE depend on whether the individual is in a graduate-dominated occupation or not?
  - Do the returns to HE vary by the subject undertaken?

Finally, Chapter 6 concludes.

CHAPTER 2
The NCDS Data

The data used in this study come from the British National Child Development Survey (NCDS), which is a continuing panel survey of all individuals born in Britain between 3 and 9 March 1958. Since birth, individuals in the NCDS have been surveyed at five different points, the most recent being the fifth wave (NCDS5) which took place in 1991 when they were 33 years old.

The NCDS data are rich in a number of aspects that make them useful for our purposes. First, they contain detailed information on the higher education qualifications achieved by each individual up to 1991. We can identify the type of qualification obtained and, for those who commenced their HE studies by 1981, the subject studied.[5] We also know whether individuals started HE as mature students (aged 21 or over) or earlier, and whether individuals who started a given course passed, failed or dropped out. Second, we have information from the 1978 school exams file in the NCDS on school qualifications. Third, we have a wealth of information on the family and school backgrounds of the children in the early years of the survey. This is used in our modelling procedure to examine the effects of different family circumstances and schooling backgrounds on HE attainment, and to control for possible biases arising from these effects when estimating the effect of HE on labour market outcomes. Fourth, the NCDS contains information on the results of maths and reading ability tests administered to the children at ages seven, 11 and 16. We use the results for ability at age seven in an attempt

---

[5]Subject information is not yet available from the NCDS5 survey.

to control for the child's 'innate' ability when estimating the effects of HE. Lastly, NCDS5 has information on employment status and hourly and weekly wages at age 33, well after most individuals complete their HE. We use these various measures of labour market outcomes in the regressions that we estimate.

2.1   Sample Selection Issues in the NCDS

The original NCDS sample contained 18,562 individuals, but a rather smaller sample than this is used for the main part of this study. This is mostly because of the choice of comparator group — we use just those who have A levels for the basis of our comparison of labour market outcomes. Our sample is also smaller than the original because we conduct our analysis only on those individuals who actually appear in the NCDS in 1991 and for whom we have adequate information about wages.

Issues arising from these sample selections are discussed in turn. In particular, we look at the choice of comparator group and the effects of panel attrition and missing information on our sample size and overall results.

The comparator group: those with at least one A level

In estimating the returns to HE, we only include those individuals who have achieved at least one A level at some time up to 1991. This is because we are interested in how labour market outcomes compare for those with HE qualifications and those who *could have* gone on to HE but did not do so.

Of around 18,500 original members of the NCDS, there are 3,264 individuals who report having passed at least one A level or Scottish Higher,[6] either at school or subsequently. For this, we draw information from the 1978 school exams file provided in the NCDS and from self-reported information from Waves 4 (1981) and 5 (1991). If at any of these points the individual reports having passed at least one A level or Scottish Higher, they are included in our sample. The first part of our formal analysis examines what sorts of individuals in NCDS5 do not obtain A levels and so never make it into our main sample.

Notice that this choice of comparator group assumes that the only way into HE is through the 'traditional route' of A levels. For those with first-degree- or higher-degree-level qualifications, this assumption is indeed borne out by the data. Although there are some individuals from the original sample who never pass any A levels but do go on to get degrees, they are relatively few. Including them in the overall sample does not significantly alter the estimated wage differences between those with degrees and those with no HE qualifications at all (see Table 2.1 and discussion below). Given that it is important for our purposes to define in some way those who have the *prospect* of going on to pass degrees and higher degrees as a basis of comparison, this sample selection suggests itself as a sound one.

For those with non-degree HE qualifications, such as nursing, some teacher training, and HNC/HND qualifications, the implications of choosing this comparator group are rather more serious. This is because there are a large number of individuals in the NCDS who do not follow the traditional route into such qualifications and

---

[6]Notice that pupils from Scotland are not treated equivalently to those from England and Wales in terms of selection into the comparator group, since five Scottish Highers are generally taken to be equivalent to three A levels (for instance, in calculating the UCCA scale — see Table A.2 in Appendix A for details).

have achieved NVQ Level 4 qualifications by 1991 without ever having passed A levels. Looking at the NCDS overall, as many as two-thirds of men who have non-degree HE qualifications by 1991, and more than half of such women, have never passed an A level. Moreover, an examination of the wage outcomes of those who do not follow the traditional route shows that they fare significantly less well in terms of wages than those who do (see Table 2.1 and discussion below).

Defining a suitable comparator group for these individuals is problematic. Since people in the NCDS appear to follow a variety of routes into this form of HE, it is very difficult to identify those who could have done other NVQ Level 4 qualifications but, for whatever reason, did not. Selecting on those who have obtained at least five O levels (or equivalent), regardless of A level attainment, does not solve the problem, since there are almost as many individuals with other NVQ Level 4 qualifications by 1991 who do not have five or more O levels as there are without any A levels.

Given the inherent problem in identifying those who could have gone on to other forms of HE besides degrees, we do not attempt to define a better comparator group for these individuals. The returns to this sort of HE qualification reported in the analysis that follows must therefore be interpreted with great care. They show the returns to HE qualifications amongst a narrow group of those who actually attain them, drawing from a sample who did relatively well at school or passed A levels after leaving school. They do not represent the return to these qualifications for those who have been less successful at school.

The implications of our choice of comparator group for individuals with different levels of HE are set out in more detail in Table 2.1. The first column of this table shows information about the number of men in our NCDS sample who have followed the 'traditional route' into HE, reporting at least one pass at A level as well as their HE qualifications. This column also gives information about the average wages of these men compared with those whose highest qualification is at A level. These wage differences were obtained by regressing the log hourly wage of employees in 1991 on dummies for their highest qualification obtained, with no other controls included. The estimated coefficients on these dummies can be interpreted as the raw average wage differential for those with HE qualifications compared with those with A levels but no HE. Coefficients that are not significant at the 10 per cent level are given in parentheses.

The second column shows the same information when the sample is expanded to include those who have followed a 'non-traditional' route into HE (that is, those who have obtained HE qualifications but have never reported any passes at A level). As can be seen from Table 2.1, the raw wage differentials for men with first degrees and higher degrees are not affected at all by the inclusion of these relatively few extra individuals in the sample. Working men with first degrees gained through the traditional route see an average premium of 20.8 per cent to their wages, and those with higher degrees see an average premium of 15.6 per cent. This is not much altered when those who follow the non-traditional route are included. The story is quite different for those whose highest qualification is non-degree HE, such as NVQ Level 4 qualifications. The size of the sample is more than tripled by the inclusion of men following non-traditional routes into these qualifications (268 to 821); the average wage difference between this group and those just with A levels drops from 15.0 per cent to 1.6 per cent when those without A levels but with non-degree HE qualifications are included amongst them.

For women, the picture is much the same. Although the raw differentials for women are higher across the

TABLE 2.1
Sample sizes and raw wage differentials:
traditional route and any route into HE compared

	Men		Women	
	Traditional route into HE	*Any route into HE*	*Traditional route into HE*	*Any route into HE*
Highest qualification non-degree HE				
Sample size	268	821	316	781
Raw wage differential	0.150	(0.016)	0.261	0.148
Highest qualification first degree				
Sample size	476	520	418	441
Raw wage differential	0.208	0.212	0.391	0.383
Highest qualification higher degree				
Sample size	209	228	177	183
Raw wage differential	0.156	0.155	0.427	0.422
Total sample				
Sample size	1,251	1,867	1,278	1,772

Notes:
Coefficients that are not significant at the 10 per cent level are given in parentheses.
Sample sizes include all individuals in each sample, regardless of employment status in 1991. Wage differentials are given just for employees in 1991.
'Traditional route into HE' sample includes just those who report having obtained at least one pass at A level any time up to 1991.
'Any route into HE' sample includes those with HE qualifications who have never obtained A levels.
Dependent variable used for raw wage differential is real log hourly wage of employees in 1991 (January 1995 prices).
Base group for raw wage differentials is all those employees in 1991 whose highest qualification is at A level.

board than those for men (this issue is discussed in detail later in this report), the inclusion of those bypassing A levels but obtaining HE qualifications has a similar effect on numbers in the sample and on the raw wage differentials. In particular, including women with non-degree HE qualifications but no A levels more than doubles the number of women with such qualifications in the sample (from 316 to 781) and reduces the wage difference between them and individuals just with A levels from 26.1 per cent to 14.8 per cent.

Panel attrition and missing wages information

Some of the original sample of the NCDS were not interviewed at the fifth wave in 1991, although they appeared in earlier waves. This could be because they have abandoned the survey altogether, or it could be because they have temporarily left and will reappear in subsequent waves. (Some of those who did not appear in Wave 4 reappeared at Wave 5.) We are unable to include these people in our analysis, since we have no information at all about their labour market outcomes in 1991. Amongst those with at least one A level, we lose 505 individuals through this panel attrition.

There are also individuals who responded to the survey in 1991 but did not provide full information about their weekly wage or hours of work (this is only a problem for those who are employees). This reduces our main sample by a further 230.

Our main sample is therefore reduced to 2,529 individuals with at least one A level, 1,251 of whom are men and 1,278 of whom are women (see Table 2.2). This is the largest possible sample on which we can conduct our basic analysis. For some of these people, other important information that is used to measure ability and family background is missing from the data. For a large proportion, information about the subject studied at HE level is not available. Rather than exclude these people from the analysis altogether, we have opted to keep them in and use missing variable dummies where appropriate in the regressions. This avoids, as far as possible, the risk that we are left with a much smaller, and possibly unbalanced, sample on which to estimate the returns to HE.

TABLE 2.2

Selection of the NCDS 'at least one A level' sample

	Sample size
Full NCDS	18,562
less No A levels passed by 1991	−15,298
less Not interviewed in 1991	−505
less Employee 1991, missing hourly wage	−230
Main sample	**2,529**

In order to assess how far both panel attrition and missing wages information in Wave 5 introduced possible bias into the composition of our main sample, we have made a detailed comparison of this sample of the NCDS and the Labour Force Survey (LFS), which is a large-scale individual-level survey that is not subject to panel attrition. This suggests that, despite some attrition from the NCDS, the composition of the remaining sample is similar to that of the LFS, in terms of the occupational structure of employment for those individuals with at least one A level.[7]

We have also compared the wages of employees in the NCDS with wages information provided in the General Household Survey (GHS) of 1991 and the British Household Panel Surveys (BHPSs) of 1991–94. In cross-sections such as these, we are unable to distinguish individuals who have followed traditional routes into HE (that is, via A levels) from others. We therefore compare the wages of employees aged 30–35 in the GHS and in the BHPS with those of the NCDS sample following *any route* into HE. Table 2.3 provides details of the comparisons, showing the number of employees at each qualification level and the raw wage mark-up to different HE qualifications. Notice that there are relatively few individuals in the GHS and BHPS who are in the same cohort as the NCDS members, and

---

[7]The 1991 LFS does not contain any wage information.

TABLE 2.3

Number of employees and raw wage differentials:
NCDS any route into HE, GHS and BHPS compared

	Men			Women		
	NCDS any route	*GHS*	*BHPS*	*NCDS any route*	*GHS*	*BHPS*
Highest qualification non-degree HE						
No. of employees	663	86	78	553	53	45
Raw wage differential	(0.015)	(0.000)	(0.079)	0.148	(0.145)	(0.042)
Highest qualification first degree						
No. of employees	414	51	137	283	42	108
Raw wage differential	0.212	0.179	0.288	0.383	0.477	0.313
Highest qualification higher degree						
No. of employees	192	2	29	137	5	12
Raw wage differential	0.155	0.289	0.346	0.422	(−0.021)	(0.536)
Total sample						
No. of employees	1,504	215	435	1,188	154	284

Notes:

Coefficients that are not significant at the 10 per cent level are given in parentheses.

Sample sizes and wage differentials cover only those who are employees in 1991.

GHS sample contains employees in the 1991 GHS aged 30–35.

BHPS sample contains employees in the 1991–94 BHPSs aged 30–35. BHPS sample regressions contain year dummies as well as HE dummies.

Dependent variable used for estimation of raw wage differential is real log hourly wage of employees in 1991 (January 1995 prices).

Base group for raw wage differentials is employees in 1991 whose highest qualification is at A level.

so some of the cell sizes in the estimation of the mark-ups to HE qualifications are extremely small. The coefficients that are not significant at the 10 per cent level are given in parentheses. Looking at the group whose highest qualification is a first degree, we see from Table 2.3 that, for men, the raw return to this qualification is somewhat lower in the GHS and somewhat higher in the BHPS than in the NCDS. For women, the raw return is higher in the GHS and lower in the BHPS than in the NCDS.

Table 2.2 summarised the sample selections made to arrive at our main sample used for the bulk of the analysis that follows. Some further results based on a smaller sample containing all those passing two or more A levels (or three or more Scottish Highers)[8] are presented in footnotes throughout the course of this report, and in tables set out in Appendix C. This sample contains 901 men and 871 women. Of these, 857 men and 658 women were in employment in 1991. Of those in employment, 731 men and 566 women were employees.

2.2 Data Description

Below, we show some descriptive statistics for our main sample of individuals with at least one pass at A level.

Educational attainment

The proportions of individuals who completed HE courses by 1991 are shown in Table 2.4. Sample sizes are given in parentheses. From this table, we see that about three-quarters of men in the 1958 cohort with A levels go on to get some kind of HE qualification by the age of 33. Just over one-fifth obtain non-degree HE qualifications as their highest qualification, whilst more than half obtain either first or higher degrees. Most of

---

[8]Three Scottish Highers are equivalent to two A levels.

TABLE 2.4

Percentage of individuals completing HE courses
(sample with at least one A level)

	Percentage not completing any HE	*Percentage completing non-degree HE qualification*	*Percentage completing first degree*	*Percentage completing higher degree*	*Total sample*
Men	24	21	38	17	100
	(298)	(268)	(476)	(209)	(1,251)
Women	29	25	33	14	100
	(367)	(316)	(418)	(177)	(1,278)
All	26	23	35	15	100
	(665)	(584)	(894)	(386)	(2,529)

Note: Sample sizes are given in parentheses.

those getting degrees stop at first-degree level: the highest qualification of 38 per cent of the sample of men is a first degree; 17 per cent of men with A levels are educated to higher-degree level.

The proportion of women with A levels who go on to get some form of HE qualification is somewhat lower than that of men. About 29 per cent of women with A levels do not go on to get any form of HE qualification at all. Almost a quarter undertake non-degree HE qualifications, reflecting the large number of women obtaining nursing and teacher training qualifications. About one-third of women with A levels complete first degrees as their highest qualification level, whilst 14 per cent obtain higher degrees by 1991.

Employment and self-employment

Table 2.5 shows the proportions of men and women in the NCDS in employment in 1991. Table 2.6 looks at the employment structure of the population by HE. In both tables, the employment category includes both employees and the self-employed. The employee/self-employed split is considered further below.

TABLE 2.5

**Percentage of individuals in employment in 1991
(sample with at least one A level)**

	Percentage in employment
Men	95
	(1,192)
Women	76
	(965)
All	85
	(2,157)

Note: Sample sizes are given in parentheses.

Table 2.5 shows that the employment rate amongst the sample of men in 1991 is very high indeed — 95 per cent are in either employment or self-employment at this time. By contrast, about three-quarters of women in this sample of those with at least one A level are in employment in 1991.

Table 2.6 shows that employment rates do not vary much between different levels of educational attainment for men, but for women the differences are much more pronounced. Only 69 per cent of women whose highest educational qualification is at A level are employed in 1991, compared with about 77 per cent amongst those with first degrees and other HE qualifications, and 81 per cent amongst those with higher degrees. This differ-

TABLE 2.6

**Percentage of individuals in employment in 1991
(sample with at least one A level)**

	Did not complete HE	*Non-degree HE*	*First degree*	*Higher degree*
Men	95	96	95	95
	(283)	(256)	(454)	(199)
Women	69	78	77	81
	(254)	(245)	(323)	(143)
All	81	86	87	89
	(537)	(501)	(777)	(342)

Note: Sample sizes are given in parentheses.

TABLE 2.7

**Percentages of workers who are employees and self-employed in 1991
(sample with at least one A level)**

	Percentage who are employees	*Percentage who are self-employed*
Men	84	16
	(1,006)	(186)
Women	86	14
	(832)	(133)
All	85	15
	(1,838)	(319)

Note: Sample sizes are given in parentheses.

ence may reflect differences in timing choices with respect to child-rearing as well as higher potential wages.

Turning to the split amongst those in some kind of employment between employees and the self-employed, Table 2.7 shows that about 84 per cent of men in employment are employees and 16 per cent self-employed in 1991. A smaller proportion (about 12 per cent) of women in employment are self-employed.

Note that when we go on to consider how the wage outcomes of those with HE qualifications differ from the wage outcomes of those without, we concentrate just on the group of employees in 1991.[9]

Wages

In Table 2.8, we examine how average wages differ between employees who completed HE courses prior to 1991 and those who did not. Our method for doing this was to regress log hourly wages on dummies for HE completion. It should be stressed that we do not include any other variables as controls in the regression at this stage, since we are initially interested in the observed wage differentials, before we control for other factors

---

[9]The NCDS5 data do not have wages information for self-employed individuals.

TABLE 2.8

Raw wage differentials
(sample with at least one A level)

	Men	*Women*
Non-degree HE	0.150	0.261
	(0.039)	(0.040)
First degree	0.208	0.391
	(0.034)	(0.038)
Higher degree	0.156	0.427
	(0.042)	(0.046)

Notes:
Standard errors are given in parentheses.
The base group is individuals with at least one A level but no HE qualifications.

that determine wages (what we term the 'raw wage differentials'). The standard errors on the estimated regression coefficients are given in parentheses in the table.

The results in Table 2.8 suggest that the average differences between the hourly wages of those with HE qualifications and those without are much larger for women than for men. Given that the figures are in logs, the results imply a raw premium of 26.1 per cent for women with non-degree HE qualifications, 39.1 per cent for women with first degrees and 42.7 per cent for women with higher degrees. For men, there is a 15 per cent raw mark-up for men with non-degree HE qualifications, 20.8 per cent for those with first degrees and 15.6 per cent for those with higher degrees. This difference between men and women largely reflects the fact that women with A levels who do not continue in HE receive substantially lower wages than men with A levels (by around 40 per cent). We look more closely at these gender differences in Chapter 5.

Note that the raw mark-up for men and women with non-degree HE qualifications compared with those without is very sensitive to the choice of comparator group. This was discussed in Section 2.1. Those individuals who obtain non-degree HE qualifications without ever obtaining A levels do not appear in our sample at all. When these people, who have followed non-traditional routes into HE, are included in the sample, the raw wage differences between them and those with just A levels drop considerably.

CHAPTER 3
Methodological Issues

3.1 Problems in Estimating the Returns to Higher Education

There are a number of problems that can affect estimates of the returns to higher education (or indeed estimates of the effect of HE on the probability of being employed). We examine these below in the context of a simple equation for the individual's hourly wage:[10]

$$(3.1) \quad w_i = \beta HE_i + \gamma' X_i + \varepsilon_i$$

where w_i is individual i's log wage, HE_i is a dummy variable indicating individual i's completion of a higher education course, X_i is a vector of other exogenous variables that might affect wages (such as age, region and job characteristics) and ε_i is a random error term. The return to HE is given by β.

Ordinary least squares (OLS) estimation of the return to HE, β, gives rise to problems because HE outcomes are unlikely to be randomly assigned across the population but are *endogenous,* being the result of unobservable individual choices, attributes and circumstances (which are contained in the error term ε_i). If we do not take this endogeneity into account, our estimates of the return to HE may be biased.[11] In particular, some of the

---

[10]We use the hourly wage in this example because (under certain assumptions about labour market competitiveness) it has a reasonably clear interpretation as a market outcome. The same estimation problems arise with the other measures of labour market outcomes considered in the report (that is, weekly wages and employment).

[11]We require $E(X_i, \varepsilon_i) = 0$ for OLS to give us an unbiased estimate of β.

most important biases that may arise when estimating equation (1) by OLS are the following:

(a) *Omitted variable bias due to unobserved ability:* Assume that individual ability has a positive effect on wages. Assume also that individual ability and HE attainment are positively correlated. If X_i does not contain a measure of ability, then there will be positive correlation between HE_i and ε_i (which will include unobserved ability), biasing estimates of β (the return to higher education) upwards.

(b) *Attenuation bias due to measurement error in* HE_i: A common feature of survey data on educational attainment is that there is measurement error in responses — that is, some people in the survey tend to report having qualifications that they did not in fact complete, and vice versa. Measurement error in the HE variable can be shown to bias estimates of the return to higher education (β) downwards. However, Dearden (1997) shows that the downward biases arising from measurement error in the NCDS education variables are not large.

(c) *Bias arising from heterogeneity in the rate of time preference over the sample:* Given that entering HE normally means that the individual forgoes the earnings he or she would have gained from work over the duration of the course, people with high rates of time preference (high discount rates) have a higher opportunity cost of entering HE, and so (other things equal) they will be less likely to enter. This can lead to downward bias in the estimates of the returns to HE if not properly controlled for (see Card (1994) and Willis and Rosen (1979)).

3.2 How Can We Correct for These Biases?

A number of approaches have been used in the literature to correct for these biases. These include within-family fixed effect estimation techniques, instrumental variable (IV) techniques, and proxy or matching methods.

Within-family fixed effect approaches

Within-family fixed effect estimation techniques use data from twins or siblings to obtain estimates of the returns to education that are free from the biases caused by the correlation of education with unobserved (and observed) family attributes. This is done by looking at *differences between siblings'* education and earnings (see Ashenfelter and Krueger (1994) and Ashenfelter and Zimmerman (1993)). The impact of fixed observed and unobserved family characteristics can be differenced out and the estimates of the returns to education will be free of biases caused by unobserved family effects that affect twins and/or siblings in identical ways. The use of these techniques is not entirely problem free, in particular since the statistical problems associated with measurement error tend to be accentuated in these models and the samples used are often small.

Instrumental variable techniques

Instrumental variable techniques use an exogenous source of variation in educational outcomes, which does not affect wage outcomes other than indirectly through its effect on education. Instruments that have been used in previous studies include changes in the compulsory minimum school-leaving age (Harmon and Walker, 1995), season of birth (Angrist and Krueger, 1992), proximity to educational institutions (Card, 1993) and sibling composition (Butcher and Case, 1994). An interesting feature of most of these studies is that the estimated return to education using IV methods is substantially higher than the returns estimated using OLS. So, for example, Harmon and Walker (1995) find that the estimated return to an extra year of schooling in the UK using the increase in the compulsory school-leaving age in 1973 as an instrument was 17 per cent, compared with an OLS estimate of around 8 per cent.

The size of the apparent downward bias in recent studies, such as Harmon and Walker's, has surprised some commentators, as it seems unlikely that such large biases are attributable solely to measurement error in the HE data. Card (1994) offers an alternative explanation of why the IV method may be producing high estimates of returns to education. He argues that many of the recent studies use instruments based on a single variable (for example, Harmon and Walker's use of the increase in the compulsory schooling age), and, furthermore, the instruments used tend only to affect individuals with a high discount rate. As discussed in Section 3.1, a high discount rate is more likely to arise for individuals from poorer backgrounds, since these households may be less able and/or willing to forgo the earnings lost from an extended course of HE and to find the resources necessary to finance such studies. It is straightforward to show that IV estimation where the instrument set is a single dummy is equivalent to estimating the returns to education for the subgroup for whom the dummy variable is 'switched on' — in the Harmon and Walker case, those individuals who would have left education at 15 had it not been for the school-leaving-age reform. If the returns to education for this subgroup are higher than for the population as a whole, then IV estimation produces results that are driven entirely by this unusually high return. Card argues that the return to education for the subgroup with a high discount rate will indeed be higher than for the population at large because those individuals will not participate in HE unless their expected future returns to doing so are relatively large (which offsets the disincentive to forgo immediate earnings arising from the high discount rate). Hence the IV results may tell us very little about average returns to education for the population as a whole.

Proxy and matching methods

The final approach that has been used in the literature to obtain unbiased estimates of the return to education is to proxy the correlated unobserved individual characteristics. These studies have tended to concentrate on omitted ability bias and have used observed measures of ability such as IQ tests and other ability tests to proxy unobserved ability (see, for example, Blackburn and Neumark (1993), Griliches and Mason (1972) and Griliches (1977)). This is equivalent to *matching* individuals on the basis of these observed measures of ability. This matching idea is discussed in more detail below. The ability to proxy unobserved determinants of education, employment and wages is clearly going to depend on the quality of the data used. The NCDS data used in this report are particularly rich in this regard.

CHAPTER 4
The Modelling Approach

Our modelling approach begins by looking at what types of individuals make it into our comparator group at all from the larger NCDS, by modelling the determinants of obtaining at least one A level for individuals who participated in NCDS5. In the remainder of the report, we concentrate only on individuals with at least one A level, looking first at the factors that are important in determining whether or not they undertake some form of higher education. Finally, we use both IV techniques and proxy and matching methods to model the impact of HE on employment and wages (both hourly and weekly). Our approach is discussed in more detail below.

4.1 Modelling A Level Attainment

Most of the analysis in this report concentrates on individuals in the NCDS cohort with at least one A level, rather than the NCDS cohort as a whole. It is interesting, therefore, to see whether individuals who complete A levels have markedly different characteristics from those individuals who do not complete at least one A level. We do this by estimating a model that looks at which factors are important in determining the probability of completing at least one A level for all individuals who participated in the NCDS5 survey of 1991. A reduced form probit equation for completion of A levels is estimated:

$$(4.1) \quad AL_i^* = \delta' Z_i + \varepsilon_i$$

where, in the simplest specification, AL_i^* is a normally distributed 'latent' variable such that $AL_i = 1$ if $AL_i^* > 0$ and $AL_i = 0$ if $AL_i^* \leq 0$. Z_i is a vector of exogenous variables that may affect selection into the A level group, comprising

- ability test variables at age seven (dummies for being in the top four quintiles of the maths and reading ability tests at age seven);
- school type at age 16 (the base is comprehensive school and/or secondary modern; dummies are included for grammar and private schools);
- region at age 16 (two dummies for Scotland and London/South-East);[12]
- father's and mother's years of education;
- father's social class in 1974;
- a dummy for the absence of the mother or father figure from the home in 1974;
- mother's employment status in 1974;
- a dummy for whether the household experienced financial difficulties in 1969 or 1974;
- the number of siblings the individual had in 1974;
- the number of *older* siblings the individual had in 1974;
- 1971 census returns information on the proportions of households in the child's local authority in 1974 where
  - the head of household was unemployed;
  - the head of household was a professional or managerial person;
  - the head of household was an unskilled worker;

---

[12]The regional dummies are included mainly to account for the fact that, in 1974, the education system was in a transitional stage, with some regions more or less fully comprehensivised and other regions retaining a significant proportion of grammar schools.

- the householders were owner-occupiers;
- the householders were council tenants.

4.2 Modelling the Determinants of Higher Education Completion

In modelling the determinants of HE completion, we take as our base group all individuals who completed at least one A level but who did not continue to any form of HE. We then distinguish between individuals who completed non-degree HE courses, those who completed a first degree and those who completed a higher degree. We then look at what factors are important in determining the probability of completing each type of HE qualification. We do this using an ordered probit maximum likelihood procedure which exploits the ordering of our HE outcomes.

Our HE outcome variable is defined as follows:

HE_i = 0 if individual i did not complete any form of HE
= 1 if individual i completed a non-degree HE course
= 2 if individual i completed a first degree
= 3 if individual i completed a higher degree.

Our reduced form ordered probit model for completion of HE is given by

$$(4.2) \quad HE_i^* = \gamma' Z_i + v_i$$

where HE_i^* is a normally distributed 'latent' variable such that $HE_i = j$ if $\mu_{j-1} < HE_i^* \le \mu_j$ where the μ_j are estimated from the model and $j = 0, 1, 2, 3$. Z_i is a vector of exogenous variables that may affect whether

HE is undertaken and comprises the variables discussed in Section 4.1.[13]

4.3 Modelling the Impact of Higher Education on Employment and Wages

From the discussion above, it is clear that the main problem encountered when attempting to estimate the impact of HE on wages and employment is controlling for the endogeneity of HE outcomes. If there are unobserved individual characteristics that determine both HE outcomes *and* employment and/or wage outcomes, then our estimates of the impact of HE on these outcomes will be biased.

In this report, we use both instrumental variables techniques and proxy methods to control for this endogeneity problem. We do not use within-family estimation methods as the number of twins in the NCDS sample by 1991 who both have A levels is very small.[14]

Instrumental variable approach

In this report, we control for unobserved ability bias by using variables derived from the scores in maths and reading ability tests that were administered to children in the NCDS at age seven as our best available measure of the child's inherent ability.[15] In addition to this, our IV approach uses a set of family background variables that we assume affect the choice to go on to HE but have no independent influence on wage or employment

---

[13]We only include dummy variables identifying individuals in the top two quintiles of the reading and mathematical ability tests, as individuals in our A level sample predominantly come from these two quintiles.

[14]There are less than 10 pairs of twins who satisfy this criterion.

[15]Ability tests were also conducted when the individuals were aged 11 and 16, but these measures are more likely to be affected by schooling and are less likely to be good measures of 'innate' ability, which is what we are attempting to measure.

outcomes once HE is controlled for, as instruments for HE. The variables we use as instruments (Q_i) are a subset of the variables Z_i described before; namely,

- father's and mother's years of education;
- father's social class in 1974;
- a dummy for the absence of the mother or father figure from the home in 1974;
- mother's employment status in 1974;
- a dummy for whether the household experienced financial difficulties in 1969 or 1974;
- the number of siblings the individual had in 1974;
- the number of *older* siblings the individual had in 1974;
- 1971 census returns information on the proportions of households in the child's local authority in 1974 where
  - the head of household was unemployed;
  - the head of household was a professional or managerial person;
  - the head of household was an unskilled worker;
  - the householders were owner-occupiers;
  - the householders were council tenants.

Our IV approach involves using the results from our earlier work to carry out two-step estimation procedures (see Heckman (1979)). For example, in estimating the impact of HE on wages (the returns to HE), we estimate the following wage equation:

$$(4.3) \quad \ln w_i = \beta_1 HE_1 + \beta_2 HE_2 + \beta_3 HE_3 + \alpha' X_i + \varsigma_h \lambda_{hi} + \varsigma_e \lambda_{ei} + e_i$$

where $HE_1 = 1$ if the person's highest qualification was a non-degree HE course and 0 otherwise, $HE_2 = 1$ if the person's highest qualification was a first degree course and 0 otherwise, and $HE_3 = 1$ if the person's highest qualification was a higher degree course and 0 other-wise. The β_j give the respective returns to each of the three qualifications, conditional on observed factors X_i and endogeneity corrections λ_{hi} and λ_{ei}. The X_i are our exogenous explanatory variables and consist of variables from our Z_i that are not in our instrument set Q_i; namely,

- ability test variables at age seven (dummies for being in the top four quintiles of the maths and reading ability tests at age seven);
- school type at age 16 (the base is comprehensive school and/or secondary modern; dummies are included for grammar and private schools);
- region at age 16 (two dummies for Scotland and London/South-East).

In some specifications, the X_i also include job characteristics, such as employer size, whether the individual's job is in the private sector and whether the individual is a union member.

In our estimation, we want to control for the fact that HE choices may be endogenous (endogeneity effect) and for the fact that we only observe wages for those individuals who are actually employed (employment selection effect). Following Heckman (1979) and Smith and Blundell (1986), we do this by including two adjustment terms — the generalised residuals or inverse Mills ratios (represented by the terms λ_{hi} and λ_{ei} in equation (4.3))[16] which correct for the endogeneity problem and the employment selection problem respectively. These terms are constructed from our reduced form HE ordered probit equation and a reduced form employment probability equation (see Appendix B for full details). If $\varsigma_e =$

---

[16]Details of how these generalised residuals are calculated are given in Appendix B.

0, then selection is not a problem; if $\varsigma_h = 0$, then endogeneity is not a problem.[17] The validity of this, and indeed any, IV procedure depends crucially on the appropriate choice of the instrument set. At least one excluded instrument is required for every inverse Mills ratio in our wage equation. In our specification, we therefore require at least two instruments. In our work, we always have more than two instruments in our Q_i; these extra instruments are called over-identifying instruments. The instruments first need to be significant explanators of HE outcomes and second must have no legitimate role in a wage equation controlling for HE. The validity of our over-identifying instruments can be tested using a Sargan test (see Sargan (1958)).

The proxy or matching approach

The instrumental variables approach relies heavily on the assumption that the variables in the instrument set do not affect labour market success once education is controlled for. If this is a poor assumption (for example, if our specification fails a Sargan test), then the results from the IV method will be subject to specification error. An alternative estimation strategy stems from the argument that the endogeneity problem in estimating the returns to HE (or the effect of HE on employment) is a consequence of missing data; namely, that typically unobserved and therefore omitted individual characteristics (ability, motivation, the rate of time preference, etc.) affect HE outcomes. Because these variables are also correlated with employment and wage outcomes, the estimates of the impact of HE on both wages and employment will be biased. The NCDS contains a wealth of data on personal and family background characteristics that we can use to proxy these typically unobserved

---

[17]The latter test is known as a Hausman endogeneity test (see Smith and Blundell (1986)).

characteristics by including them on the right-hand side of both the wage and employment equations. If it can be convincingly argued that the unobserved factors are adequately proxied in the data, then this proxy approach is less restrictive than the IV approach in that we do not restrict the causal impact of the proxy variables on labour market outcomes as only operating through educational performance. If, however, our proxy variables still fail to capture important unobserved characteristics, then our estimates could still be biased.

The proxy technique for estimating the wage equation (and the employment equation as well) simply involves including all our exogenous variables (Z_i) as regressors in the wage equation (and the employment equation):

$$(4.4) \quad \ln w_i = \beta_1 HE_1 + \beta_2 HE_2 + \beta_3 HE_3 + \varphi' Z_i + \eta_i$$

where the β_j give the respective returns to each of the three qualifications *conditional* on Z_i. This is analogous to matching our sample on Z_i and assuming common return parameters β_j. In this context, $\varphi' Z_i$ can be interpreted as the matching function.

Extensions to the modelling procedure

(a) *Early and late starters:* One interesting extension is to consider whether the returns to HE differ according to whether the student started his or her degree immediately or soon after leaving school, or whether he or she was a 'late starter' (defined as 21 years or older). The NCDS data allow us to identify whether or not an individual started his or her first course of HE as a mature student. We exploit this by including a dummy for late starters in the employment and wage equations.

(b) *The impact of including A level scores and ability tests at 16 in our explanatory variable set:* In the initial specification of equation (4.2), the set of exogenous variables, Z_i, includes only family background variables and ability test scores when the child was very young. From the 1978 school exams file, we are able to construct individuals' A level 'score' according to the UCCA formula (where five points are awarded for each 'A' grade at A level, 4 for each 'B' grade, and so on down to 1 point for an 'E' grade pass, up to a maximum of 15 points).[18] From our NCDS3 data, we can also construct variables measuring reading and mathematical ability at the age of 16 (similar to those constructed at the age of seven). This information from somewhat later in the individual's school career may also help us to measure the effects of family background and differing ability which are typically unobserved in standard cross-sections. On the other hand, it can be argued that both the A level score and ability test results at 16 are likely to be highly endogenous to an individual's HE, wage and employment outcomes. Pupils setting their sights on going on to HE are likely to work harder towards obtaining better A level grades than those who do not — this is particularly likely to be the case since an individual's UCCA score is used as an entry requirement into HE in a lot of cases. None the less, we do experiment with specifications that include both A level scores and ability test scores at 16 to see how these affect our estimated returns.

(c) *Heterogeneous returns by ability group and family background:* The problem of bias in the estimates of

---

[18]See Appendix A for full details. This score is not available for those individuals who completed A levels after 1978. For these individuals, we include a missing UCCA score dummy variable.

returns to HE due to unobserved ability was discussed in the last section. A related issue is whether people of different levels of ability experience different returns to HE. On one hand, it is possible that HE acts as an equalising force, in that people of lower ability gain more from HE in terms of potential productivity in the labour market than do those of higher ability. On the other hand, it could be argued that individuals of higher ability are more able to exploit the opportunities for personal advancement offered by HE than are those of lower ability. It is also possible that people from different family backgrounds obtain different returns to their qualifications. We examine the possibility of heterogeneity in returns by interacting the ability test score and parents' social class variables in Z_i with the HE variables.

(d) *Returns to different subject groups:* It is possible that the returns to HE differ by subject. We explore this possibility by disaggregating HE qualifications into different subject groups as shown below:

- *Arts:* English, other languages, history, other arts subjects
- *Engineering:* engineering, technology
- *Education*
- *Social sciences:*
  – *economics, accountancy and law*
  – *other social sciences:* geography, other social science and social studies courses
- *Sciences:*
  – *maths, physics*
  – *chemistry, biology, geology, environmental science*
  – *other sciences*
- *Other subjects:* medicine, other health qualifications, agricultural qualifications, other professional/vocational qualifications, creative arts

(e) *The effect of graduate jobs:* An interesting question is whether graduates are capable of securing a return to their HE regardless of which occupation they enter, or whether the returns depend on entering 'graduate jobs' (where a graduate occupation is defined as one where a high proportion of the people doing the job are graduates). The answer to this question is interesting from a policy point of view, as well as from the perspective of understanding how the UK labour market operates and how wage differentials are generated. We investigate this question by looking at how (if at all) the returns to graduates in non-graduate jobs differ from the returns to those in the standard graduate occupations (defined as Standard Occupational Classification (SOC) categories 1 or 2), once other factors are controlled for.

CHAPTER 5
Results

5.1 The Characteristics of Individuals with A Level Qualifications

Most of the results we present for the determinants of higher education attainments are based on the subsample of people in the NCDS who had one or more (alternatively, two or more) A levels.[19] Tables 5.1 and 5.2 set out the factors affecting the probability of A level attainment amongst all those individuals who participated in NCDS5 in 1991. The *marginal effects* shown in these tables represent the estimated percentage point increase (or decrease) in the probability of achieving A levels associated with each variable.

Table 5.1 shows that, for men in the NCDS, there is a clear positive relationship between good performance in reading ability and maths tests at age seven and attaining A level qualifications. This association exists for both sorts of tests although the relationship seems to be stronger for the reading ability tests. A person who was in the top quintile of the reading ability test at the age of seven was 33.5 percentage points more likely to complete A levels than somebody who was in the bottom quintile. The respective figure for women was 31.9 percentage points, as shown in Table 5.2. Meanwhile, family background is also important. Individually, the education of both father and mother is positively related

---

[19]In all the tables that follow, we report the results from the 1+ A level sample. We refer to the results from the 2+ sample in the course of our discussion. Selected results from the 2+ sample are presented in Appendix C.

TABLE 5.1

Factors affecting the probability of A level attainment — men

Variable	Marginal effect	
Individual variables:		
Maths ability tests aged 7		
: top quintile	0.1580	**
: 4th quintile	0.0951	**
: 3rd quintile	0.0844	**
: 2nd quintile	0.0347	
Reading ability tests aged 7		
: top quintile	0.3350	**
: 4th quintile	0.2727	**
: 3rd quintile	0.1491	**
: 2nd quintile	0.0708	**
No. of siblings, 1974	−0.0235	**
No. of older siblings, 1974	0.0013	
Region, 1974		
: London	0.0426	**
: Scotland	0.1427	**
Less than 1 week off school, 1974	0.0784	**
School type, 1974		
: grammar	0.2567	**
: private	0.3984	**
Family background variables:		
Father's years of education	0.0270	**
Mother's years of education	0.0222	**
Father's social class		
: professional	0.0439	*
: skilled worker	−0.0146	
Mother in employment, 1974	−0.0138	
No father figure, 1974	−0.0233	
No mother figure, 1974	−0.0896	*
Bad financial situation, 1969/74	−0.0437	**
P-value, likelihood ratio test — family background vars.	0.000	**
P-value, likelihood ratio test — demographic vars.	0.000	**
No. of observations	5,144	
Pseudo R^2	0.2655	
Mean of dependent variable	0.243	
Predicted probability (at mean)	0.185	

Note: Dependent variable is at least one A level obtained by 1991.
* indicates significance at the 10 per cent level.
** indicates significance at the 5 per cent level.

TABLE 5.2

Factors affecting the probability of A level attainment — women

Variable	Marginal effect
Individual variables:	
Maths ability tests aged 7	
: top quintile	0.2009 **
: 4th quintile	0.1106 **
: 3rd quintile	0.1216 **
: 2nd quintile	0.2889
Reading ability tests aged 7	
: top quintile	0.3191 **
: 4th quintile	0.2458 **
: 3rd quintile	0.1499 **
: 2nd quintile	0.0891 **
No. of siblings, 1974	−0.0094
No. of older siblings, 1974	−0.0167 **
Region, 1974	
: London	0.0269
: Scotland	0.2633 **
Less than 1 week off school, 1974	0.0952 **
School type, 1974	
: grammar	0.2435 **
: private	0.2061 **
Family background variables:	
Father's years of education	0.0193 **
Mother's years of education	0.0394 **
Father's social class	
: professional	0.0931 **
: skilled worker	0.0134
Mother in employment, 1974	−0.0007
No father figure, 1974	0.0239
No mother figure, 1974	−0.0307 *
Bad financial situation, 1969/74	−0.0612 **
P-value, likelihood ratio test — family background vars.	0.000 **
P-value, likelihood ratio test — demographic vars.	0.000 **
No. of observations	5,310
Pseudo R^2	0.2747
Mean of dependent variable	0.241
Predicted probability (at mean)	0.174

Note: Dependent variable is at least one A level obtained by 1991.
* indicates significance at the 10 per cent level.
** indicates significance at the 5% level.

to A level success, as is the dummy variable for the father being in a professional or managerial social class. Conversely, dummies for the absence of a mother figure in the household in 1974, and for the household being in financial difficulties in 1969 or 1974, seem to reduce the likelihood of A level success. Other significant factors associated with men's A level performance include school type (being in a grammar school or private school in 1974 are both positively correlated with A level success) and the number of brothers or sisters in the household. For every additional child in the family, the probability of completing A levels decreased by 2.4 percentage points for men. Family size is not important for women; however, birth order is, with girls higher in the birth order more likely to complete A levels than girls lower in the birth order (controlling for family size). The demographic variables are also significant when tested jointly for both men and women (their individual values are not shown in the tables). An additional point to note is that children located in Scotland seem to be much more likely to progress to 'Highers' (the Scottish A level equivalent) than are children in England and Wales to progress to A levels.

5.2 Who Obtains Higher Education Qualifications?

Next we present the results of the equations that were run to examine the characteristics of those who obtain HE qualifications. Tables 5.3 and 5.4 present the results from our ordered probit maximum likelihood procedure. The tables report the *marginal effects* of the regressors on the probability of being in one of four states evaluated at the mean of the regressors in the data. Thus the numbers in the top line of Table 5.3 give the marginal effects of being in the top quintile of maths ability tests at age seven on the likelihood of completing different levels of higher education. So, for example, a marginal effect of −0.064 in the 'No HE' column implies that being in the top quintile of the maths test distribution means that someone would be 6.4 percentage points less likely than those in the bottom three quintiles to complete no higher education courses whatsoever. At the same time, a marginal effect of 0.029 in the 'First degree' column means that the same person would be 2.9 percentage points more likely than those in the bottom three quintiles to have completed at most a first degree. The marginal effects along a row must sum to zero (ignoring rounding effects), as being more likely to end up in one state means that someone is correspondingly less likely to end up in another state.

Table 5.3 presents the results of the determinants of different types of HE qualifications for men. Being in the top quintile of the maths score distribution at age seven is associated with a higher chance of completing a first or higher degree and with a lower chance of only having completed a non-degree HE course or no course at all. This is also true for being in the top quintile of reading ability tests. The second-top quintile of ability test score is also significant (at the 10 per cent level) for maths tests but not for reading ability.

The only other significant characteristics of the NCDS men themselves in the ordered probit are the number of siblings and the number of older siblings each had in 1974. Interestingly, a higher number of siblings is associated with better educational attainment for men. Thus while men from larger families are less likely to undertake A levels (see Table 5.1), among those who obtain A levels they are more likely to continue on to HE. Being higher in the birth order (fewer older siblings) increases the probability of men completing HE (controlling for family size).

Most of the family background variables in the ordered probit specification fail to be significant for men when considered individually. The exceptions are the

TABLE 5.3

The determinants of levels of attainment in higher education: results from ordered probit — men

Variable	No HE	Marginal effects			
		Non-degree HE course	First degree	Higher degree	
Individual variables:					
Maths ability tests aged 7					
: top quintile	–0.064	–0.024	0.029	0.058	**
: 4th quintile	–0.044	–0.015	0.021	0.038	*
Reading ability tests aged 7					
: top quintile	–0.060	–0.022	0.028	0.054	**
: 4th quintile	–0.031	–0.011	0.015	0.026	
No. of siblings, 1974	–0.019	–0.006	0.010	0.015	*
No. of older siblings, 1974	0.022	0.007	–0.011	–0.017	*
Region, 1974					
: London	0.030	0.008	–0.016	–0.022	
: Scotland	–0.000	–0.000	0.000	0.000	
Less than 1 wk off school, 1974	–0.008	–0.002	0.004	0.006	
School type, 1974					
: grammar	–0.019	–0.006	0.009	0.016	
: private	–0.013	–0.004	0.006	0.011	
Family background variables:					
Father's years of education	–0.012	–0.004	0.006	0.009	**
Mother's years of education	–0.003	–0.000	0.002	0.002	
Father's social class					
: professional	–0.037	–0.013	0.018	0.032	
: skilled worker	–0.010	–0.003	0.005	0.008	
Mother in employment, 1974	–0.026	–0.008	0.013	0.021	
No father figure, 1974	0.050	0.013	–0.028	–0.035	
No mother figure, 1974	0.028	0.008	–0.015	–0.021	
Bad financial situation, 1969/74	0.081	0.019	–0.044	–0.056	**
P-value, likelihood ratio test — family background vars.		0.001 **			
P-value, likelihood ratio test — demographic vars.		0.010 **			
No. of observations		1,251			
Pseudo R^2		0.0245			

Note: Dependent variable is highest educational qualification by 1991.
* indicates significance at the 10 per cent level.
** indicates significance at the 5 per cent level.

education of the father (which has a small positive impact on the likelihood of achieving a first or higher degree) and the household's being in a bad financial situation in 1969 or 1974 (which has a more substantial negative impact). However, the family background variables are strongly significant in a joint significance test. The demographic variables that are used as additional instruments in the employment and wage equations that we present below are also jointly significant for men.

Examination of the results in Table 5.4 for women shows a similar pattern to that for men for the influence of ability test scores on HE attainment. However, the other individual variables appear to affect HE very differently for women from the way in which they affect men. The sibling variables for women are not significant determinants of HE. On the other hand, women who were educated in Scotland seem to be more than 5 percentage points less likely to complete a first degree than women elsewhere, a difference which does not exist for men. A good school attendance record in 1974 is associated with being more likely to enter HE for women but not for men. Also, women who went to a grammar school or private school seem to be more likely to enter HE than those who went to comprehensive or secondary modern schools, whereas this difference does not seem to hold for men.

In the case of the family background variables, there is an interesting difference between the results for men and women. Mother's education is an important determinant of female educational performance, whereas father's education is not significant; for men, the reverse is true. None of the other family background variables is individually significant for women, though they are jointly significant for men and women. The additional demographic variables are not significant for women.

TABLE 5.4

**The determinants of levels of attainment in higher education:
results from ordered probit — women**

Variable	*No HE*	Marginal effects			
		Non-degree HE course	*First degree*	*Higher degree*	
Individual variables:					
Maths ability tests aged 7					
: top quintile	−0.094	−0.027	0.052	0.069	**
: 4th quintile	−0.070	−0.018	0.039	0.049	**
Reading ability tests aged 7					
: top quintile	−0.064	−0.016	0.036	0.044	**
: 4th quintile	−0.041	−0.009	0.023	0.027	
No. of siblings, 1974	0.015	0.003	−0.009	−0.009	
No. of older siblings, 1974	−0.018	−0.003	0.010	0.011	
Region, 1974					
: London	−0.016	−0.003	0.009	0.010	
: Scotland	0.084	0.010	−0.051	−0.043	**
Less than 1 wk off school, 1974	−0.048	−0.010	0.028	0.031	**
School type, 1974					
: grammar	−0.078	−0.022	0.042	0.057	**
: private	−0.075	−0.022	0.041	0.056	**
Family background variables:					
Father's years of education	−0.008	−0.002	0.005	0.005	
Mother's years of education	−0.021	−0.004	0.012	0.013	**
Father's social class					
: professional	−0.018	−0.004	0.011	0.012	
: skilled worker	0.014	0.003	−0.008	−0.008	
Mother in employment, 1974	−0.010	−0.002	0.006	0.006	
No father figure, 1974	−0.040	−0.010	0.023	0.027	
No mother figure, 1974	0.038	0.006	−0.022	−0.022	
Bad financial situation, 1969/74	0.052	0.008	−0.031	−0.029	
P-value, likelihood ratio test — family background vars.		0.000 **			
P-value, likelihood ratio test — demographic vars.		0.791			
No. of observations		1,278			
Pseudo R^2		0.0401			

Note: Dependent variable is highest educational qualification by 1991.
** indicates significance at the 5 per cent level.

5.3 The Impact of Higher Education on Employment at Age 33

Reflecting the fact that nearly all of our sample of men with at least one A level are in employment at age 33, HE is not associated with men's employment prospects. However, it appears to be an important determinant of employment for women. More-highly-educated women are considerably *more* likely to be in employment at 33 than those whose highest qualification is at A level.

Tables 5.5 and 5.6 show results from the estimation of probit equations on the probability of being in employment in 1991. The results for four different specifications of the employment equation are presented. These equations have been estimated for men and women separately.

Specification 1 includes HE dummies only as explanatory variables, with no other controls included. The first column of each table therefore shows the average raw difference in the predicted probability of employment by HE attainment.

The other specifications contain further explanatory variables, in order to assess the impact of HE on employment once these other factors have been controlled for. Specification 2 contains a set of basic controls, including dummies for performance in school tests at age seven as a measure of ability, region at age 16 and school type at age 16. Specifications 3 and 4 include a fuller set of controls, following the 'proxy method' approach described in Chapter 4. Specification 3 includes family background and local demographic characteristics at age 16 in addition to the basic set of controls, whilst specification 4 contains the full set of explanatory variables in specification 3 together with scores in tests at school at age 16 and A level scores.

For women, the decision to have children will have an important bearing on employment status. Although

BOX 5.1

Employment equation specifications

1. Higher education dummies only

2. As in specification 1
   + Quintiles of maths and reading ability test scores at age seven
   + Region at age 16
   + School type at age 16
   (+ Children variables for women)

3. As in specification 2
   + Family background variables (father's and mother's education,
   father's social class, mother's employment, absence of mother/father,
   number of siblings, number of older siblings, all in 1974)
   + Demographic variables (proportion of households in local authority
   with unemployed head of household, head of household in top social
   class, council tenancy, owner-occupation)
   + Good school attendance in 1974

4. As in specification 3
   + Ability test scores at age 16
   + A level score according to UCCA formula

the relationship between childbearing, HE choices and employment outcomes is not a straightforward one, since typically these things are determined jointly, we have included the number of children aged 0–4 and aged 5 and over in the set of right-hand-side variables in specifications 2, 3 and 4 of the women's employment probits. Full details of the various specifications are contained in Box 5.1.

We have also estimated the impact of HE on employment using instrumental variable techniques.[20] The results from the IV approach tended to be very similar to the results from the proxy methods presented below. Given that the richness of the data in the NCDS provides a good source of information to use in the proxy method, and that there are some doubts as to whether

---

[20] This is done by including the prediction index from our ordered HE probits in our employment probits using specification 2 (see Mallar (1977)).

TABLE 5.5

Effect of higher education on men's probability of employment at 33

Variable	Specification			
	1	*2*	*3*	*4*
Non-degree HE qualification	0.003	0.003	−0.001	−0.002
First degree	0.003	0.001	−0.007	−0.006
Higher degree	0.001	−0.002	−0.004	0.001
UCCA score				−0.001
P-value, LR test — ability at 7		0.564	0.480	0.426
P-value, LR test — ability at 16				0.107
P-value, LR test — family vars.			0.199	0.144
P-value, LR test — demographics			0.520	0.479
No. of observations	1,251	1,251	1,251	1,251
Pseudo R^2	0.000	0.023	0.085	0.108
Mean of dependent variable	0.9528	0.9528	0.9528	0.9528
Predicted probability (at mean)	0.9529	0.9562	0.9643	0.9679

Notes:
Dependent variable is employment in 1991.
LR test is likelihood ratio test.

the exclusion restriction necessary to undertake IV estimation is actually valid in this case,[21] we do not report results from IV estimation, preferring to concentrate on the proxy method.[22] This is also true for the wage equations that we present in the next subsection.

Table 5.5 shows that, for men, HE has no significant impact on the probability of employment in any of the specifications used. Indeed, none of these male employment regressions achieves any significant explanatory power. This is because of the very high employment rate amongst men with at least A levels at age 33. This means that our sample of those not in employment is very small.

The regressions on women's employment have considerably more explanatory power. HE comes in as an important factor in determining women's employment

---

[21]Indeed, Sargan tests of the over-identifying restrictions in the IV approach indicated that they were not valid in many cases. The same was true for the wage equations presented later.

[22]Full results are available from the authors.

TABLE 5.6

Effect of higher education on women's probability of employment at 33

Variable	Specification			
	1	*2*	*3*	*4*
Non-degree HE qualification	0.076 **	0.074 **	0.735 **	0.075 **
First degree	0.075 **	0.084 **	0.805 **	0.085 **
Higher degree	0.104 **	0.110 **	0.104 **	0.110 **
UCCA score				−0.004
P-value, LR test — ability at 7		0.400	0.332	0.303
P-value, LR test — ability at 16				0.612
P-value, LR test — family vars.			0.312	0.338
P-value, LR test — demographics			0.730	0.772
Number of children aged 0–4		−0.034 **	−0.033 *	−0.033 *
No. of observations	1,278	1,278	1,278	1,278
Pseudo R^2	0.008	0.019	0.035	0.038
Mean of dependent variable	0.7551	0.7551	0.7551	0.7551
Predicted probability (at mean)	0.7569	0.7593	0.7641	0.7646

Notes:
Dependent variable is employment in 1991.
LR test is likelihood ratio test.
* indicates significance at the 10 per cent level
** indicates significance at the 5 per cent level.

outcomes in each of the four specifications. Those with non-degree HE qualifications are, on average, around 7.5 percentage points more likely to be in employment at age 33 than those with just A levels. (For the 2+ A levels sample, the figure is 8.7 percentage points.) This is true in each of the specifications used.

Before controlling for any other determining factors, women with first degrees are also about 7.5 percentage points more likely to be in employment than the base group; introducing controls increases the predicted impact of HE somewhat, to over 8 percentage points. (The figure for the 2+ A levels sample is somewhat higher, at 11.2 percentage points.) Of all the controls introduced, it is those that take into account the presence of young children in the family which have the most explanatory power in these regressions. The presence of young children is associated with a significantly lower probability of being in employment at age 33.

Those women whose highest qualification is a higher degree are the most likely to be in work at age 33. Women with higher degrees are, on average, between 10 and 11 percentage points more likely to be in employment than those with just A levels. (Amongst the 2+ A levels sample, the figure is around 15 percentage points in all specifications.) This is stable across different specifications of the employment equation.

It is interesting to note that test scores at school, family background variables, and local demographic conditions at 16 are never important determinants of employment outcomes for women or men.

5.4 The Impact of Higher Education on Wages at Age 33

The relationship between various types of HE qualification and wages as measured in 1991 was estimated under a variety of different specifications. Tables 5.7 and 5.8 show how the estimated returns to different levels of HE change as we include wider groups of control variables. Specification 1 in the left-hand column shows the raw returns with no controls. Specification 2 adds ability scores at age seven and region and school type at age 16. Specification 3 adds family background variables, demographic controls from the 1971 census and characteristics of the individual's job in 1991; this corresponds to the basic 'proxy' approach outlined previously in Chapter 4. Our aim here is to control for unobserved characteristics that might affect both HE outcomes and wages by using a rich set of observable information. Finally, specification 4 includes A level scores and ability tests at age 16, in an attempt to ascertain whether including earlier measures of educational attainment and aptitude diminishes our estimates of the impact of HE on

BOX 5.2

Wage equation specifications

1. Higher education dummies only
2. As in specification 1 + Quintiles of maths and reading ability test scores at age seven + Region at age 16 + School type at age 16
3. As in specification 2 + Family background variables (father's and mother's education, father's social class, mother's employment, absence of mother/father, number of siblings, number of older siblings, all in 1974) + Demographic variables (proportion of households in local authority with unemployed head of household, head of household in top social class, council tenancy, owner-occupation) + Good school attendance in 1974 + Employer characteristics in 1991 (employer size, union membership dummy, private sector dummy)
4. As in specification 3 + Ability test scores at age 16 + A level score according to UCCA formula

wages. Box 5.2 gives details of the different specifications.

Table 5.7 shows raw returns for men of around 15 per cent to a non-degree HE qualification, 21 per cent for a first degree and just over 15 per cent for a higher degree. (The respective figures for the 2+ A levels sample are 13 per cent, 16 per cent and 10 per cent — see Table 5.7(a) in Appendix C.) Including controls for ability tests at seven, region and school type reduces the returns to degrees slightly, but has no appreciable impact on returns to non-degree courses. An F-test of the ability variables indicates that they are jointly significant. When family background and demographic variables are included, amongst others, to proxy unobserved individual characteristics that might bias the estimates of the returns, there is little change to the estimates. Neither the family background nor the demographic variables are significant. However, additional variables included to capture characteristics of the individual's job in 1991 which might exert an influence on wages (employer size dummies, union status and a public/private sector dummy) are highly significant in a joint test. When A level scores and ability tests at age 16 are included, in specification 4, they are both significant at the 5 per cent level; the returns to first and higher degrees are reduced (from 17.1 per cent to 12.2 per cent and from 14.4 per cent to 8.4 per cent respectively) but are still statistically significant. Hence, even given the fact that there is likely to be a high correlation between individuals' A level scores and their decisions and opportunities to go into HE, an average return to a first degree of around 12 per cent remains even after controlling for A level score. A person with an UCCA score of 10 out of 15 will earn, on average, around 12 per cent more than someone with a score of zero, regardless of whether they go on to HE or not.

For women, the raw returns to each level of HE in the first column of Table 5.8 appear to be considerably

TABLE 5.7

Effect of higher education on men's hourly wages at 33

	Specification			
Variable	*1*	*2*	*3*	*4*
Non-degree HE qualification	0.150 **	0.155 **	0.144 **	0.136 **
First degree	0.208 **	0.184 **	0.171 **	0.122 **
Higher degree	0.156 **	0.141 **	0.144 **	0.084 **
UCCA score				0.012 **
P-value, F-test — ability at 7		0.020 **	0.068 *	0.204
P-value, F-test — ability at 16				0.014 **
P-value, F-test — family vars.			0.109	0.228
P-value, F-test — demographics			0.236	0.178
P-value, F-test — employer vars.			0.000 **	0.000 **
No. of observations	1,006	1,006	1,006	1,006
Adjusted R^2	0.0333	0.0515	0.0913	0.1133

Note: Dependent variable is real log hourly wage in 1991 (January 1995 prices).
* indicates significance at the 10 per cent level.
** indicates significance at the 5 per cent level.

51

TABLE 5.8

Effect of higher education on women's hourly wages at 33

Variable	Specification			
	1	*2*	*3*	*4*
Non-degree HE qualification	0.261 **	0.272 **	0.223 **	0.218 **
First degree	0.391 **	0.384 **	0.368 **	0.337 **
Higher degree	0.427 **	0.408 **	0.368 **	0.319 **
UCCA score				0.011 **
P-value, F-test — ability at 7		0.289	0.693	0.821
P-value, F-test — ability at 16				0.299
P-value, F-test — family vars.			0.179	0.145
P-value, F-test — demographics			0.060 *	0.092 *
P-value, F-test — employer vars.			0.000 **	0.000 **
No. of observations	832	832	832	832
Adjusted R^2	0.1328	0.1397	0.1941	0.2067

Note: Dependent variable is real log hourly wage in 1991 (January 1995 prices).
* indicates significance at the 10 per cent level.
** indicates significance at the 5 per cent level.

higher than those for men — around 26 per cent, 39 per cent and 43 per cent for non-degree HE courses, first degrees and higher degrees respectively. (The respective figures for the 2+ A levels sample are 25 per cent, 35 per cent and 36 per cent — see Table 5.8(a) in Appendix C.) Including ability tests at seven, region and school type dummies affects the returns only slightly. The proxy approach in specification 3, including family background variables and demographics, lowers the returns to 22 per cent for non-degree courses, 37 per cent (still only a marginal reduction) for first degrees and 37 per cent (a larger reduction) for higher degrees. Including the fullest set of available controls by adding tests at 16 and A level score to the regressor set lowers the estimated returns even more (especially for higher degrees), but the returns to HE still appear highly significant and much higher than the returns for men. A woman with an UCCA score of 10 out of 15 will receive, on average, an additional return of 11 per cent over someone with a score of zero.

The main conclusions from Tables 5.7 and 5.8 are: first, that there are significant and substantial raw wage premiums for typical graduates, much of which persist even after controlling for other factors; and second, that there seem to be large differences in the returns between men and women. We examine the possible explanations of the male–female differentials later in this chapter; next, however, we analyse the patterns of returns to degrees by subject group, the effects on wages of failing a HE course, the effects of starting a HE course at the age of 21 or older, and the role of labour market experience as an explanation of the observed differentials.

5.5 Extensions to the Analysis of the Impact of Higher Education on Wages

Returns by subject category

An important extension to the analysis of the returns to HE conducted above involves considering whether the returns are different depending on the subject of the HE course that a person took. Tables 5.9 and 5.10 consider the different returns by subject for men and women respectively. The returns to different subjects have been estimated using specifications 3 and 4 of the wage equation (see Box 5.2). Splitting our sample by subject necessarily means that the sample size in each subject category is generally quite small, which means that the precision of our estimates of returns by subject is generally quite poor.

Table 5.9 shows that, in so far as we do find significant results, it appears that men completing a HE qualification in biology, chemistry, environmental sciences or geography have substantially lower returns to HE than the base group (those graduates for whom no information was available in the NCDS on the subject they took). The inclusion of A level scores in the wage equation (specification 4) does not eliminate this difference.

TABLE 5.9

Effects of degree subject, degree failure and starting late on men's hourly wages at 33

Variable	Specification 3	Specification 4
Non-degree HE qualification	0.153 **	0.142 **
First degree	0.146 **	0.099 **
Higher degree	0.142 **	0.079 *
UCCA score		0.010 **
Degree subject:		
Arts	−0.102	−0.034
Engineering	0.060	0.031
Education	0.036	0.040
Economics/accountancy/law	0.104	0.078
Other social sciences	0.065	0.063
Maths/physics	0.092	0.050
Chemistry/biology etc.	−0.170 **	−0.175 **
Other sciences	0.070	0.051
Other subjects	−0.107	−0.116 *
Failed HE course	−0.094 *	−0.129 **
Started HE course aged 21 years +	−0.078 *	−0.069 *
No. of observations	1,006	1,006
Adjusted R^2	0.1062	0.1272

Notes:
Dependent variable is real log hourly wage in 1991 (January 1995 prices).
Base subject group is missing subject information.
* indicates significance at the 10 per cent level
** indicates significance at the 5 per cent level

For women (see Table 5.10), the pattern is somewhat different: higher returns appear to be achieved in education, economics, accountancy and law, and the 'other social sciences' category. Again, the inclusion of performance at A level does not dramatically alter the results.

One explanation of these differences could be that we are picking up the effects of different standards of *intake* into the different degree subjects. For example, it seems quite plausible that better A level results are needed to gain entry to an accountancy or law course than to a chemistry or biology course. On the other hand, the

TABLE 5.10

Effects of degree subject, degree failure and starting late on women's hourly wages at 33

Variable	Specification 3	Specification 4
Non-degree HE qualification	0.206 **	0.193 **
First degree	0.321 **	0.288 **
Higher degree	0.349 **	0.296 **
UCCA score		0.010 **
Degree subject:		
Arts	0.055	0.045
Engineering	0.217	0.197
Education	0.093 *	0.100 **
Economics/accountancy/law	0.242 **	0.274 **
Other social sciences	0.106 *	0.097
Maths/physics	0.162	0.166
Chemistry/biology etc.	−0.116	−0.115
Other sciences	0.102	0.000
Other subjects	0.008	0.013
Failed HE course	−0.007	−0.016
Started HE course aged 21 years +	−0.011	0.006
No. of observations	832	832
Adjusted R^2	0.2083	0.2206

Notes:
Dependent variable is real log hourly wage in 1991 (January 1995 prices).
Base subject group is missing subject information.
* indicates significance at the 10 per cent level
** indicates significance at the 5 per cent level.

proxy approach adopted ought to control for such differences in the quality of workers; in addition, the controls for A level score included in specification 4 did not much alter the pattern of estimated returns across subjects. Another explanation is that studying in a subject with a high estimated return increases the graduate's potential productivity more than studying in a subject with a lower estimated return.

The effects of failure and starting late

The regressions from which the results in Tables 5.9 and 5.10 are taken included a control for whether individuals in the sample had started but failed to complete a HE course. In addition, a dummy was included for those who completed their first HE course but started it when aged 21 years or older. This allowed us to examine, first, whether there was any return to a HE course that was not completed, and, second, whether the returns measured at age 33 for 'mature students' were different from those for students who started their first course soon after leaving school.

Table 5.9 indicates that, for men, there seems to be a *negative* return to non-completion of a HE course: men who started but did not complete such a course had at least 9 per cent lower wages on average than those who never attempted a HE course, controlling for other factors. There are a number of potential explanations for why non-completion of a course might be negatively related to labour market performance in a regression such as this. One is that time spent on a HE course is time out of the labour market, and therefore individuals who undertook all or part of a course are likely to have lower levels of labour market experience, and hence lower wages, than those who did not undertake a course. Another possibility is that the people who did not complete courses are 'worse' than the base group with respect to some unobserved characteristic(s) (for example, motivation) and so the negative return to non-completion reflects this. It should be borne in mind that the regression in Table 5.9 contains all the proxies for such unobserved characteristics that were in specification 3 of Table 5.7 earlier, so if the proxies are satisfactory, there should not be a negative effect of non-completion in the regression due to such unobservables. Another possibility is that the penalty on non-completion reflects the negative signal that such poor performance in HE sends to employers — this is the converse of the standard 'signalling' model of HE (see, for example, Spence (1973)). This is certainly a possible interpretation of the result. However, for women, we find no evidence that those who did not complete HE courses do any worse than the base group.

As for the effect of starting HE late, men who start late seem to have an average return of 7 or 8 per cent less than those who undertook HE courses earlier. However, this still means that there is a significant positive return to HE, even for late starters. The lower returns to late starters might simply be a consequence of the fact that, as they will have entered (or re-entered) the labour market later than the early starters, they may not have built up as much recent labour market experience and so their returns may be lower. Alternatively, it might be that courses that are started late are qualitatively different from the earlier courses. For women, we find no evidence that those who started HE courses later do any worse than the base group.

The effects of controlling for labour market experience and part-time jobs

Given that we have considered the role of differential labour market experience in accounting for differences in returns for late starters compared with early starters and for those who did not complete courses compared with the group who never went into HE, it seems natural to consider the effects of putting labour market experience and part-time status into the regression as explanatory variables. There are obvious endogeneity problems involved in doing this, as experience and part-time status are partially determined both by the amount of HE undertaken and by the wages on offer to individuals. However, it is interesting to see how the inclusion of these variables affects the measured returns (see Table 5.11).

Experience appears to be positively related to wage levels for both men and women. The coefficients imply that an extra year of experience implies a wage premium

TABLE 5.11

Effects of labour market experience on hourly wages

Variable	Specification 3 Men	Women
Non-degree HE qualification	0.153 **	0.270 **
First degree	0.259 **	0.496 **
Higher degree	0.267 **	0.547 **
Labour market experience	0.033 **	0.054 **
Part-time	0.103	−0.098 **
No. of observations	1,006	832
Adjusted R^2	0.1122	0.3022

Note: Dependent variable is real log hourly wage in 1991 (January 1995 prices).
** indicates significance at the 5 per cent level.

of 3 per cent for men and 5 per cent for women. Women in part-time jobs receive, on average, almost 10 per cent lower wages than women in full-time jobs. Comparing the results in Table 5.11 with the earlier returns to HE in the absence of controls for experience and part-time status in Tables 5.7 and 5.8, it seems clear that including these variables in the regression increases the estimated returns to HE, especially the returns to a degree. This reflects the fact that, on average, people who undertook HE courses will have had time out of the labour market whilst doing the course and hence they will be less experienced, *ceteris paribus*, than individuals who did not undertake such a course.

Do the returns to higher education differ according to ability or family background?

In the analysis thus far, we have assumed that the financial returns to HE qualifications are the same across people of different ability and family background. In order to examine the possibility of heterogeneity of returns across different sorts of people, we have interacted test score variables[23] and father's social class variables[24] with the HE terms and introduced these interactions as extra regressors in our wage equation. The coefficients on the interaction terms show any additional return to HE for people of high ability or higher father's social class. The coefficients on all of these interaction terms are of very small magnitude and none is statistically significant (so they are not reported here). This suggests that the returns to HE qualifications do not vary according to background or ability.

Differences in the returns by occupation: do 'graduate jobs' matter?

An important extension to the analysis presented so far involves assessing whether the average returns to HE that we find in the earlier wage equation specifications apply for all types of employment that graduates might consider, or whether the pay-offs are partially or wholly dependent on being in a 'graduate job' (that is, a job in an occupation dominated by graduates). Table 5.12 examines this by interacting the returns to HE with a dummy for whether the graduate is in SOC 1 or 2 (the professional or managerial occupations).[25] This means that the base group in the regression is now the group of individuals who did not complete any form of HE *and*

---

[23]We defined somebody to be of high ability if they were in the top quintile of both the reading and maths tests at the age of seven or they were in the fourth quintile of one of the tests and the top quintile of the other test. This high ability dummy variable was then interacted with the HE dummy variables.

[24]We defined somebody as coming from a favourable social background if their father was in a managerial or professional occupation when they were aged 16. This dummy variable was then interacted with the HE dummy variables.

[25]These two occupations were chosen as they were the only two dummy variables that were significant when we included occupational dummy variables in our wage equation.

TABLE 5.12

Higher education and wages at 33: differential effects by occupation

Variable	Men		Women	
	Base coefficient	*Additional, SOC 1 or 2*	*Base coefficient*	*Additional, SOC 1 or 2*
No HE qualification	(0)	0.135 **	(0)	0.312 **
Non-degree HE qualification	0.155 **	0.076	0.238 **	0.186 **
First degree	0.143 **	0.132 **	0.278 **	0.263 **
Higher degree	0.191 **	0.009	0.364 **	0.109 **
No. of observations		1,006		832
Adjusted R^2		0.1406		0.2873

Notes:
Dependent variable is real log hourly wage in 1991 (January 1995 prices).
Base group is individuals with no HE qualifications who are not in SOC 1 or 2.
The results are for specification 3 (see Box 5.2).
** indicates significance at the 5 per cent level.

were not in SOC 1 or 2. The specification of the wage equation used is specification 3 (see Box 5.2).

The results of interacting the returns to HE with the dummy for SOC 1 or 2 show that, for men, there is a significant additional pay-off to being in a professional or managerial occupation of around 13 per cent for those with a first degree. The additional pay-off to non-degree courses and higher degrees is lower and not statistically significant. For women, there are significant additional pay-offs to being in SOC 1 or 2 for all three HE categories; the pattern of returns is similar to that for men, with the additional pay-off for those with a first degree being higher than the pay-off for those with a non-degree course, which is in turn higher than the addition to those with a higher degree. Both the basic returns to different types of HE and the additional returns to being in the top occupational groups are higher for women than for men. It is also interesting that there seems to be a mark-up to being in a graduate occupation even for individuals with no HE qualification (the top row of Table 5.12).

The evidence from Table 5.12 is that there do seem to be higher returns to being in SOC 1 or 2, at least for graduates whose highest degree was at undergraduate level, and in the case of women there are higher returns for all graduates. This finding raises the question of what is causing the graduate job effect. In a purely competitive model of the labour market, there should be no differences in equilibrium between remuneration for equally productive individuals in one occupation as opposed to another. If we believe that the simple competitive model is a good representation of the way the labour market actually works, then there are two main explanations of the graduate job effect. One hinges on unobserved factors that affect productivity: the graduates in non-graduate occupations may be simply less productive than the graduates in graduate jobs (similarly, the non-graduates in non-graduate occupations may also be less productive than the non-graduates who make it into graduate jobs). If this were the true explanation of the results, it would cast doubt on the validity of our 'proxy' approach to modelling the returns, as the family background and demographic variables in the regression are meant to control for relevant unobserved characteristics. Short of having measures of productivity in the job that are more direct than the wage, there is no way of testing this explanation. The other competitive hypothesis would relate to compensating differentials — that is, the idea that the observed wage is not an adequate measure of overall remuneration. The explanation of the graduate job effect here would be that both sets of graduates are equally productive but the graduates in non-graduate occupations receive higher non-wage remuneration (pensions, benefits in kind, improvements to the workplace environment, etc.) than those in graduate jobs. This explanation seems unlikely, because casual observation would suggest that the professional and managerial occupations are at least as likely to carry non-wage benefits as other occupations (if not more so). An alternative explanation which also hinges on compensating differentials is that graduates in professional and managerial occupations may be paid more than those similarly qualified in different occupations because their jobs are more stressful or demanding.

The alternative to these competitive explanations of the graduate job effect is that the results are picking up real differences in returns to HE between individuals of similar attributes which persist across occupations because the labour market does not fully conform to the standard competitive model. For example, it might be that jobs in many professional or managerial occupations attract rents due to imperfect competition or monopoly power, or that labour market frictions and imperfect information mean that professional and managerial jobs are often allocated in 'internal labour markets', isolated to some extent from competitive forces. Discriminating between alternative explanations of these graduate job effects should be a priority for additional research in this field.

Gender wage differentials and the returns to higher education

In analysing the results presented so far, it has been noted that a consistent feature of the estimated returns to HE is that they appear to be higher for women than for men. In this section, we analyse how differences in the returns to HE by gender affect the 'gender earnings gap' which is a prominent feature of UK data on earnings (as documented by, for example, Harkness (1996)). The regressions reported in Table 5.13 are run on a pooled sample of men and women. The HE variables are interacted with male dummies to examine whether there are significant gaps between men's and women's hourly

TABLE 5.13

Gender wage differentials for different higher education groups

Variable	Specification 1	Specification 3
Basic return from:		
Non-degree HE qualification	0.261 **	0.229 **
First degree	0.391 **	0.363 **
Higher degree	0.427 **	0.366 **
Additional return for men from:		
A level	0.380 **	0.426 **
Non-degree HE qualification	0.269 **	0.338 **
First degree	0.197 **	0.233 **
Higher degree	0.109 **	0.207 **
P-value, F-test — ability at 7		0.042 **
P-value, F-test — family background vars.		0.114
P-value, F-test — demographics		0.033 **
P-value, F-test — employer variables		0.000 **
No. of observations	1,838	1,838
Adjusted R^2	0.1532	0.2086

Notes:
Dependent variable is real log hourly wage in 1991 (January 1995 prices).
Base group is women with A levels.
Family variables, school variables and employer variables are fully interacted with gender in specification 3.
** indicates significance at the 5 per cent level.

wage levels by education group. A raw specification with no controls (specification 1) is considered, followed by a regression with a set of control variables and proxies for unobservable characteristics (specification 3). In specification 3, variables that relate to employer and job characteristics, family background and school type are also interacted with gender.

Table 5.13 shows that there is a gender wage gap of 38 per cent between men and women with no HE qualifications in the raw specification. For the sub-groups of people with HE qualifications, there are *smaller* earnings gaps, and the gaps *decrease* the further up the education distribution we go, to a minimum of under 11 per cent between men and women with higher degrees. When we control for ability, family background, demographics and employer characteristics, the estimated gender wage gap increases at all education levels. This indicates that, if anything, the raw differential under-states the true extent of differences between the earnings of similarly-qualified men and women. None the less, the finding that the gap is smaller for more-highly-educated groups is an interesting result.

If we attribute differences in wages between simi-larly-qualified men and women to 'unfair' discrimina-tion, then the narrowing of the gap at higher education levels might indicate that it is more difficult for employ-ers to discriminate in jobs that attract graduates. An al-ternative hypothesis is that the observed gender earnings gap is due to differences in the characteristics of men and women which affect productivity but which are not controlled for in our regression specification. One pos-sibility is that men are more experienced than women, due to women spending time out of the labour force to have children. But even when a control for experience was included in the regression specification, a substan-tial earnings gap persisted. Another possibility is that there are differences in unobservable characteristics (for example, motivation) between men and women which account for the gap. Even if this were the case, the proxy approach in specification 3 is designed to control for it as much as possible, and the persistence of an unex-plained earnings gap under this hypothesis would indi-cate the failure of the proxy approach.

A third possibility is that the earnings gap can be explained by compensating differentials. To be credible, this explanation would have to involve some feature of women's work which is not controlled for in the regres-sion as it stands, but which is valuable to women and thus facilitates the paying of lower wages to women than to men. One possible feature of women's work that might fulfil this role is the fact that part-time working is widespread among women. To explain the gender wage gap as a compensating differential in this context, one would have to argue that women valued the flexibility of part-time work as opposed to full-time work, and hence that controlling for part-time status in the wage equation would substantially change the results. From Table 5.11 earlier, we see that it is true that female part-timers have almost 10 per cent lower hourly wages than female full-timers, on average. However, even if we were to make the (strong) assumption that this 10 per cent gap wholly reflects a compensating differential for part-time work, this would leave a large proportion of the earnings gap unexplained (particularly as women with HE qualifications are less likely to be part-timers than less-educated women).

We conclude in this section that there is a substantial gap between male and female hourly earnings which is not easily explained by competitive theories of labour remuneration, but which seems to be narrower for men and women with HE than for those with just A levels.

Weekly wages

The wage equation specifications shown above all use the log *hourly* wage as the dependent variable. An alternative is to consider the *weekly* wage. The results from weekly wage equations with and without controls and proxies for unobserved factors (specifications 1 and 3 respectively) are shown in Tables 5.14 and 5.15.

Table 5.14 shows that, for men, the estimated weekly returns to HE are slightly higher than, but similar to, the hourly returns shown in Table 5.7 under both specification 1 and specification 3. (Table 5.14(a) in Appendix C shows the results for the 2+ A levels sample.) For women, the pattern is different: considering weekly wages instead of hourly wages (Table 5.15) reduces the estimated return for those with non-degree qualifications (from 22.3 per cent to 16.8 per cent in the proxy specification), but increases it by 2 percentage points in the

TABLE 5.14

Effect of higher education on male weekly wages at 33

Variable	Specification			
	1	*2*	*3*	*4*
Non-degree HE qualification	0.172 **	0.180 **	0.160 **	0.150 **
First degree	0.222 **	0.192 **	0.171 **	0.122 **
Higher degree	0.177 **	0.160 **	0.165 **	0.103 **
UCCA score				0.126 **
P-value, F-test — ability at 7		0.027 **	0.123	0.285
P-value, F-test — ability at 16				0.015 **
P-value, F-test — family vars.			0.158	0.315
P-value, F-test — demographics			0.105	0.058 *
P-value, F-test — employer vars.			0.000 **	0.000 **
No. of observations	1,006	1,006	1,006	1,006
Adjusted R^2	0.0330	0.0647	0.1425	0.1629

Notes:
Dependent variable is real log *weekly* wage in 1991 (January 1995 prices).
Explanatory variables as described in Box 5.2.
* indicates significance at the 10 per cent level.
** indicates significance at the 5 per cent level.

TABLE 5.15

Effect of higher education on female weekly wages at 33

Variable	Specification			
	1	*2*	*3*	*4*
Non-degree HE qualification	0.240 **	0.243 **	0.168 **	0.169 **
First degree	0.421 **	0.411 **	0.388 **	0.403 **
Higher degree	0.533 **	0.518 **	0.456 **	0.465 **
UCCA score				0.087
P-value, F-test — ability at 7		0.352	0.636	0.573
P-value, F-test — ability at 16				0.460
P-value, F-test — family vars.			0.124	0.102
P-value, F-test — demographics			0.021 **	0.031 **
P-value, F-test — employer vars.			0.000 **	0.000 **
No. of observations	832	832	832	832
Adjusted R^2	0.0610	0.0610	0.1447	0.1511

Notes:
Dependent variable is real log *weekly* wage in 1991 (January 1995 prices).
Explanatory variables as described in Box 5.2.
** indicates significance at the 5 per cent level.

case of first degrees and by around 9 percentage points in the case of higher degrees. These changes in the returns when considering weekly wages largely reflect differences in the number of hours worked by sections of the population with HE qualifications compared with the base group of individuals with A levels but no HE. So, for example, if individuals with first degrees work longer hours than the base group, we would expect estimates of the returns based on weekly wages to be higher than estimates based on hourly wages.

CHAPTER 6
Conclusions

This report has compared a group of British men and women born in March 1958 who undertook some form of higher education prior to 1991 with a corresponding group who obtained one or more A levels at school but, despite this, did not proceed into HE. This comparison aimed to answer two main sets of questions. One was 'what are the determinants of entry into higher education?'. It was found that pupils who showed high ability at a young age at school were more likely to become graduates than others. At the same time, individuals from more educated or more affluent family backgrounds were also more likely to go on to obtain HE qualifications. Moreover, family background was an important determinant of getting A level qualifications in the first place.

The second group of questions that we set out to answer was concerned with the impact of various types of HE on wages and employment prospects in 1991. Examining the returns to men and women in their early thirties has the advantage that this cohort has potentially been in the labour market long enough after graduation for their full returns to be measured. The returns were estimated using a 'proxy' or 'matching' approach which attempted to control for possible biases to the regression estimates induced by unobserved individual characteristics. This was achieved by including a whole range of individual and family background variables in the NCDS that might reasonably be expected to proxy the unobservables.

For men, there was no discernible evidence of an effect of HE on employment; this was because, regardless of qualifications obtained, there were very few men in the sample who were not in employment at age 33. For women, it was found that graduates were significantly more likely to be in employment at age 33 than their non-graduate counterparts. The results for the effects of HE attainment on hourly wage levels showed that there were average 'raw' returns to an undergraduate degree of around 21 per cent for men and 39 per cent for women. Controlling for ability at age seven, region, school type, family background, demographic characteristics and various other features of the job (for example, employer size and unionisation) reduced the estimated return to around 17 per cent for men and 37 per cent for women. None the less, it is clear that the returns appear substantial even when controlling for other factors. The returns to higher degrees and non-degree HE courses were generally lower than those to undergraduate degrees, but still statistically significant.

Towards the end of the report, we attempted to investigate various subsidiary issues concerning the impact of HE on wages and produced some interesting findings. In particular, we found that the gender earnings gap was lower between men and women at various levels of higher educational attainment than it was between men and women with just A levels. A substantial gap remained which did not appear to be fully explained by either differences in experience between men and women or differences in hours of work. Another interesting result was the finding of large wage premiums for graduates in occupations classified in SOCs 1 and 2, compared with graduates outside these occupational groupings. It was found that failure in a HE course seemed to be related to lower wages for men but not for women. Similarly, men who started their first HE course at the age of 21 or older seemed to have lower wages than those who started before the age of 21, controlling for other factors.

The evidence from this report of reasonably large private financial returns to HE qualifications for the cohort now in their late thirties has some interesting potential policy implications. If today's graduates will be able to secure similar returns, then it may be deemed feasible to expect future graduates to contribute a larger share of the costs of HE themselves. On the other hand, HE produces a more highly skilled and productive work-force, and this may entail social returns as well as the private returns measured in this report. The huge expansion in participation in HE in recent years should serve to place such issues high up on any policy-making agenda.

APPENDIX A
Definitions

TABLE A.1

Higher education qualification definitions

Qualification	Definition
Higher degree	All higher degree qualifications
First degree	First degree
Other non-degree higher education	Non-degree NVQ Level 4: HNC/HND, BEC/TEC higher, university diploma or certificate, professional or nursing qualifications, HE diploma or certificate, C&G full technological certificate or insignia award in technology
A level	A level qualification or Scottish Higher

TABLE A.2

UCCA scale

Grade at:	Points on the UCCA scale
A level	A=5, B=4, C=3, D=2, E=1 If more than three A levels, best three results counted
Scottish Higher	A=3, B=2, C=1 If more than five Highers, best five results counted

APPENDIX B
Technical Details of the Modelling Approach

Generalised Residuals for IV Approach

In estimating the impact of higher education on wages (the returns to higher education), we estimate the following wage equation:

$$(B.1) \quad \ln w_i = \beta_1 HE_1 + \beta_2 HE_2 + \beta_3 HE_3 + \alpha' X_i + \varsigma_h \lambda_{hi}$$
$$+ \varsigma_e \lambda_{ei} + e_i.$$

This contains two *generalised residual* terms to control for endogeneity:

(a) *The correction for the endogeneity of higher education:* This is produced by running the ordered probit

$$(B.2) \quad HE_i^* = \gamma' Z_i + \varepsilon_i$$

where HE_i^* is a normally distributed 'latent' variable such that $HE_i = j$ if $\mu_{j-1} < HE_i^* \leq \mu_j$ where the μ_j are estimated from the model and $j = 0, 1, 2, 3$. Z_i is a vector of exogenous variables that may affect whether higher education is undertaken, and comprises the variables discussed in Section 4.1. Following Heckman (1979), the inverse Mills ratio (generalised residual) is constructed as

$$(B.3) \quad \lambda_{hi} = \frac{\phi(\hat{\mu}_j - Z_i' \hat{\gamma}) - \phi(\hat{\mu}_{j+1} - Z_i' \hat{\gamma})}{\Phi(\hat{\mu}_j - Z_i' \hat{\gamma}) - \Phi(\hat{\mu}_{j+1} - Z_i' \hat{\gamma})}$$

where ϕ is the normal probability distribution function (pdf), Φ is the normal cumulative distribution function (cdf) and $\hat{\mu}$ and $\hat{\gamma}$ are the estimated coefficients from the higher education ordered probit equation.

(b) *The correction for selection into employment:* This is produced by running the reduced form employment probit equation

$$(\text{B.4}) \quad E_i^* = \psi' Z_i + u_i$$

where E_i^* is a normally distributed 'latent' variable such that $E_i = 1$ if $E_i^* \geq 0$ and $E_i = 0$ if $E_i^* < 0$. The inverse Mills ratio or selection adjustment term is given by

$$(\text{B.5}) \quad \lambda_{ei} = \frac{\phi(\hat{\psi}Z_i)}{\Phi(\hat{\psi}Z_i)}$$

where ϕ is the normal pdf, Φ is the normal cdf and $\hat{\psi}$ are the estimated coefficients from the employment probit equation.

APPENDIX C
Selected Additional Regression Results

TABLE 5.7(a)

Effect of higher education on men's hourly wages at 33
(sample with 2 or more A levels)

Variable	Specification			
	1	2	3	4
Non-degree HE qualification	0.132 **	0.144 **	0.129 **	0.107 **
First degree	0.160 **	0.150 **	0.143 **	0.106 **
Higher degree	0.099 **	0.099 **	0.116 **	0.067
UCCA score				0.012 **
P-value, F-test — ability at 7		0.368	0.521	0.510
P-value, F-test — ability at 16				0.023 **
P-value, F-test — family vars.			0.021 **	0.075 *
P-value, F-test — demographics			0.447	0.337
P-value, F-test — employer vars.			0.000 **	0.000 **
No. of observations	731	731	731	731
Adjusted R^2	0.0148	0.0358	0.0764	0.0998

Note: Dependent variable is real log hourly wage in 1991 (January 1995 prices).
* indicates significance at the 10 per cent level.
** indicates significance at the 5 per cent level.

TABLE 5.8(a)

Effect of higher education on women's hourly wages at 33
(sample with 2 or more A levels)

Variable	Specification			
	1	2	3	4
Non-degree HE qualification	0.248 **	0.247 **	0.210 **	0.213 **
First degree	0.346 **	0.345 **	0.335 **	0.326 **
Higher degree	0.361 **	0.345 **	0.308 **	0.279 **
UCCA score				0.010 **
P-value, F-test — ability at 7		0.366	0.800	0.901
P-value, F-test — ability at 16				0.207
P-value, F-test — family vars.			0.418	0.397
P-value, F-test — demographics			0.061 *	0.066 *
P-value, F-test — employer vars.			0.000 **	0.000 **
No. of observations	566	566	566	566
Adjusted R^2	0.0781	0.0873	0.1360	0.1508

Note: Dependent variable is real log hourly wage in 1991 (January 1995 prices).
* indicates significance at the 10 per cent level.
** indicates significance at the 5 per cent level.

TABLE 5.14(a)

Effect of higher education on men's weekly wages at 33
(sample with 2 or more A levels)

Variable	Specification			
	1	*2*	*3*	*4*
Non-degree HE qualification	0.182 **	0.199 **	0.165 **	0.137 **
First degree	0.191 **	0.181 **	0.165 **	0.123 **
Higher degree	0.133 **	0.138 **	0.159 **	0.102 *
UCCA score				0.014 **
P-value, F-test — ability at 7		0.423	0.629	0.491
P-value, F-test — ability at 16				0.010 **
P-value, F-test — family vars.			0.029 **	0.116
P-value, F-test — demographics			0.323	0.163
P-value, F-test — employer vars.			0.000 **	0.000 **
No. of observations	731	731	731	731
Adjusted R^2	0.0194	0.0382	0.1317	0.1579

Notes:
Dependent variable is real log *weekly* wage in 1991 (January 1995 prices).
Explanatory variables as described in Box 5.2.
* indicates significance at the 10 per cent level.
** indicates significance at the 5 per cent level.

TABLE 5.15(a)

Effect of higher education on women's weekly wages at 33
(sample with 2 or more A levels)

Variable	Specification			
	1	*2*	*3*	*4*
Non-degree HE qualification	0.185 *	0.175	0.114	0.109
First degree	0.299 **	0.292 **	0.299 **	0.312 **
Higher degree	0.421 **	0.404 **	0.356 **	0.364 **
UCCA score				–0.004
P-value, F-test — ability at 7		0.415	0.933	0.845
P-value, F-test — ability at 16				0.326
P-value, F-test — family vars.			0.474	0.467
P-value, F-test — demographics			0.048 **	0.065 *
P-value, F-test — employer vars.			0.000 **	0.000 **
No. of observations	566	566	566	566
Adjusted R^2	0.0319	0.0211	0.1173	0.1212

Notes:
Dependent variable is real log *weekly* wage in 1991 (January 1995 prices).
Explanatory variables as described in Box 5.2.
* indicates significance at the 10 per cent level.
** indicates significance at the 5 per cent level.

REFERENCES

Angrist, J. D. and Krueger, A. B. (1992), 'Estimating the payoff to schooling using the Vietnam-era draft lottery', National Bureau of Economic Research, Working Paper no. 4067.

Ashenfelter, O. and Krueger, A. B. (1994), 'Estimates of the economic returns to schooling from a new sample of twins', *American Economic Review*, vol. 84, pp. 1157–73.

— and Zimmerman, D. (1993), 'Estimates of the returns to schooling from sibling data: fathers, sons and brothers', Princeton University, Industrial Relations Section, Working Paper no. 318.

Blackburn, M. L. and Neumark, D. (1993), 'Omitted ability bias and the increase in the return to schooling', *Journal of Labour Economics*, vol. 11, pp. 521–43.

Bryson, A. and Lissenburgh, S. (1996), 'The returns to graduation', Department for Education and Employment, Research Study no. RS15.

Butcher, K. and Case, A. (1994), 'The effect of sibling sex composition on women's education and earnings', *Quarterly Journal of Economics*, vol. 109, pp. 531–63.

Card, D. (1993), 'Using geographic variation in college proximity to estimate the return to schooling', National Bureau of Economic Research, Working Paper no. 4483.

— (1994), 'Earnings, schooling and ability revisited', National Bureau of Economic Research, Working Paper no. 4832.

Dearden, L. (1997), 'Ability, families, education and earnings in Britain', Institute for Fiscal Studies, Working Paper, forthcoming.

Department for Education and Employment (1996), *Departmental Report*, London: HMSO.

Griliches, Z. (1977), 'Estimating the returns to schooling: some econometric problems', *Econometrica*, vol. 45, pp. 1–22.

—— and Mason, W. (1972), 'Education, income and ability', *Journal of Political Economy*, vol. 80, pp. S74–S103.

Harkness, S. (1996), "The gender earnings gap: evidence from the UK', *Fiscal Studies*, vol. 17, no. 2, pp. 1–36.

Harmon, C. and Walker, I. (1995), "Estimates of the economic return to schooling for the UK', *American Economic Review*, vol. 85, pp. 1278–86.

Heckman, J. J. (1979), 'Sample selection bias as a specification error', *Econometrica*, vol. 47, pp. 153–61.

Mallar, C. D. (1977), 'The estimation of simultaneous probit models', *Econometrica*, vol. 45, pp. 1717–22.

Sargan, J. D. (1958), 'The estimation of economic relationships using instrumental variables', *Econometrica*, vol. 26, pp. 393–415.

Smith, R. and Blundell, R. W. (1986), 'An exogeneity test for a simultaneous tobit model with an application to labour supply', *Econometrica*, vol. 54, pp. 679–85.

Spence, M. (1973), 'Job market signalling', *Quarterly Journal of Economics*, vol. 87, pp. 355–74.

Willis, R. J. and Rosen, S. (1979), 'Education and self-selection', *Journal of Political Economy*, vol. 87, pp. S1–S36.